First World War
and Army of Occupation
War Diary
France, Belgium and Germany

23 DIVISION
Divisional Troops
102 Field Company Royal Engineers
25 August 1915 - 31 October 1917

WO95/2177/2

The Naval & Military Press Ltd
www.nmarchive.com
Published in association with The National Archives

Published by

The Naval & Military Press Ltd

Unit 10 Ridgewood Industrial Park,

Uckfield, East Sussex,

TN22 5QE England

Tel: +44 (0) 1825 749494

www.naval-military-press.com

www.nmarchive.com

This diary has been reprinted in facsimile from the original. Any imperfections are inevitably reproduced and the quality may fall short of modern type and cartographic standards.

© **Crown Copyright**
Images reproduced by permission of The National Archives, London, England, 2015.

Contents

Document type	Place/Title	Date From	Date To
Heading	WO95/2177/2		
Miscellaneous	23rd Division 102nd Field Coy. R.E. Aug 1915-197 Oct To Italy		
Heading	23rd Division 102 F.C.R.E. Vol :I Aug Sept & Oct 15 Jan 19 121/7517		
Heading	CRE 23rd Division Herewith War Diary for Aug. Sep. Oct.1915 For Transmission to DAG GHQ 3 Echelon 4/11/15		
War Diary	Bordon Hants	25/08/1915	13/09/1915
War Diary	Erquinghem	15/09/1915	25/10/1915
Heading	23rd Division 102nd F.C.R.E. Vol 2 121/7624 Nov 15		
War Diary	War Diary Of 102nd Field Coy From 1.XI 15 To 30 XI 15 (Volume II)		
War Diary	Erquinghem	02/11/1915	29/11/1915
War Diary		25/11/1915	25/11/1915
Heading	23rd Division 102nd R.E. Vol.3 121/7921		
War Diary	Erquinghem	12/12/1915	27/12/1915
War Diary	Erquinghem-LYS	31/12/1915	31/12/1915
War Diary	102nd F.C.R.E. Vol 4		
War Diary	Erquinghem	01/01/1916	31/01/1916
Heading	102 F.C.R.E. Vol 6		
War Diary	Erquinghem	06/02/1916	21/02/1916
War Diary	Vieux Berquin	22/02/1916	22/02/1916
War Diary	Steenbecque	23/02/1916	29/02/1916
War Diary	Camblain Chatelain	01/03/1916	07/03/1916
War Diary	Ablain-St-Nazaire	08/03/1916	13/03/1916
War Diary	Ruitz	14/03/1916	16/03/1916
War Diary	Fosse X	17/03/1916	01/04/1916
War Diary	Petit Sains	12/04/1916	22/04/1916
War Diary	Forse X	23/04/1916	23/04/1916
War Diary	Sains	24/04/1916	30/04/1916
War Diary	Ruitz	01/05/1916	09/05/1916
War Diary	Fosse X Near	10/05/1916	10/05/1916
War Diary	Sains En Gohelle	12/05/1916	18/05/1916
War Diary	Bully	19/05/1916	12/06/1916
War Diary	LA Thieuloye	13/06/1916	15/06/1916
War Diary	Verchin Matringhem	17/06/1916	22/06/1916
War Diary	Matringhem	23/06/1916	24/06/1916
War Diary	Berguette Station	25/06/1916	25/06/1916
War Diary	Longueau	25/06/1916	25/06/1916
War Diary	Yseux	26/06/1916	30/06/1916
Heading	War Diary Of 102nd Coy R.E. From 1st July 1916 To 31st July 1916		
War Diary	Allonville	01/07/1916	02/07/1916
War Diary	Lahoussoye	02/07/1916	03/07/1916
War Diary	Henencourt	04/07/1916	04/07/1916
War Diary	Dernancourt	05/07/1916	12/07/1916
War Diary	Frechencourt	13/07/1916	21/07/1916
War Diary	Millencourt	22/07/1916	27/07/1916
War Diary	Becourt Wood	28/07/1916	31/07/1916

Heading	23rd Division Engineers 102nd Field Company R.E. August 1916		
War Diary	Vol 11 War Diary Of 102nd (Field) Company R.E. From 1st August 1916 To 31st August 1916		
War Diary	Becourt Wood	01/08/1916	08/08/1916
War Diary	Behencourt	09/08/1916	11/08/1916
War Diary	Famechon	12/08/1916	13/08/1916
War Diary	Longpre Bailleul	14/08/1916	14/08/1916
War Diary	Fletre	15/08/1916	16/08/1916
War Diary	Doudou Farm	17/08/1916	31/08/1916
Heading	War Diary Of 102nd FD Coy R.E. From Sept 1st 1916 To Sept 30th 1916		
War Diary	Doudou Farm	01/09/1916	03/09/1916
War Diary	Fletre	04/09/1916	05/09/1916
War Diary	Basse-Boulogne	06/09/1916	10/09/1916
War Diary	Arques Saleux	11/09/1916	11/09/1916
War Diary	Allonville	12/09/1916	12/09/1916
War Diary	Bresle	13/09/1916	19/09/1916
War Diary	Shelter Wood	19/09/1916	09/10/1916
War Diary	Albert	10/10/1916	12/10/1916
War Diary	Famechon	13/10/1916	13/10/1916
War Diary	St. Riquier	14/10/1916	16/10/1916
War Diary	R.E. Camp On Reninghelst-Vlamertinghe Road	17/10/1916	22/10/1916
Heading	War Diary November 102nd Fd Coy. R.E. Vol 14		
War Diary	R.E. Camp On Road	01/11/1916	30/11/1916
War Diary	Ouderdom-Vlamertinghe	15/11/1916	29/11/1916
Heading	War Diary Of 102nd Field Coy R.E. For Month Of December		
War Diary	R.E. Camp On road	01/12/1916	31/12/1916
War Diary	Ouderdom Vlamertinghe	07/12/1916	31/12/1916
Heading	War Diary Of 102nd Coy R.E. From January 1st 1917 to January 31st 1917		
War Diary	R.E. Camp on Ouderdom Vlamertinghe Road	01/01/1916	28/01/1916
Heading	War Diary Of 102nd Field Coy R.E. From 1st February 1917- 28 February 1917 Volume 55 & 56		
War Diary	R.E. Camp on Ouderdom-Vlamertinghe Road	01/02/1916	24/02/1916
War Diary	Lederzeele	25/02/1916	25/02/1916
War Diary	Bayenghem	26/02/1916	26/02/1916
War Diary	Tournehem	27/02/1916	19/03/1916
War Diary	Bayenghem Les Eperlecques	20/03/1916	20/03/1916
War Diary	Broxeele	21/03/1916	21/03/1916
War Diary	Bambecque	22/03/1916	31/03/1916
War Diary	Ledrenghem	01/04/1916	04/04/1916
War Diary	Watou Area	06/04/1916	06/04/1916
War Diary	Reninghelst Area	07/04/1916	07/04/1916
War Diary	Belgian Chateau	08/04/1916	16/04/1916
War Diary	Ypres	17/04/1916	01/05/1916
War Diary	Winnipeg Camp	02/05/1916	02/05/1916
War Diary	Boeschepe	03/05/1916	10/05/1916
War Diary	Ypres	11/05/1916	31/05/1916
War Diary	Ypres	01/06/1917	07/06/1917
War Diary	Hill 60	07/06/1917	12/06/1917
War Diary	Ypres	12/06/1917	15/06/1917
War Diary	Dickebusch	15/06/1917	16/06/1917
War Diary	Berthen Area	17/06/1917	28/06/1917
War Diary	Dickebusch & Spoil Bank	29/06/1917	04/07/1917

War Diary	Larch Wood Tunnels	05/07/1917	21/07/1917
War Diary	Dickebusch	22/07/1917	22/07/1917
War Diary	Berthen Area	23/07/1917	25/07/1917
War Diary	Zutove	26/07/1917	29/07/1917
War Diary	Lumbres	30/07/1917	07/08/1917
War Diary	Vlamertinghe Area	08/08/1917	25/08/1917
War Diary	Dickebusch	26/08/1917	23/09/1917
War Diary	Dickebusch Area	24/09/1917	24/09/1917
War Diary	La Clytte Area	25/09/1917	10/10/1917
War Diary	Ridge Wood	12/10/1917	21/10/1917
War Diary	Boeshepe Area	22/10/1917	31/10/1917

No 95/2177/2

23RD DIVISION

102ND FIELD COY. R.E.
AUG 1915 - JAN 1919.
1917 OCT

TO ITALY

121/7517

23rd Kuraini

10 2w̅ F.C.R.E.
Vol: I
Aug Sep & Oct 15
Jan 19

CRE 23rd Division.

CONFIDENTIAL

Herewith WAR DIARY for Aug. Sept. Oct. 1915
for transmission to A a q GHQ 3rd Echelon.

4/11/15

C B Bonham
Maj. RE
OC 102nd Fd.Co. RE

23 Div

Army Form C. 2118

(1)

Instructions regarding War Diaries and Intelligence Summaries are contained in F. S. Regs., Part II. and the Staff Manual respectively. Title pages will be prepared in manuscript.

WAR DIARY
or
INTELLIGENCE SUMMARY.
(Erase heading not required.)

102nd Fd. Co. R.E. from 25.8.15

Place	Date	Hour	Summary of Events and Information	Remarks and references to Appendices
Bordon Hants	25/8/15	9.0 p.m. 10.0 p.m.	Right Half Company paraded – entrained for Southampton at 11.5 pm & arrived 1.30 am 25th Left Half Company " " " " at 12.5 am 25th " 2.30 am " Strength 6 Officers – 222 NCO's & men	
	26/8/15		Half in Custom Shed at docks = embarked in S.S. "Australind" at 5.0 pm (except about 2 Offr & 45 NCO & men who went by "Empress Queen" (set off about 5.30 pm = nearly rammed by following transport off CHISNOT – (6 ft off our stern) – picked up by destroyer off Spit Head – v. calm passage.	
	27/8/15	2.30 am 10.0 am 4.0 pm	Arrived off HAVRE. Entered harbour & disembarked = Marched to Rest Camp no 5	
	28/8/15	9.0 am 2.45 pm 6.0 pm 7.30 pm	Left Camp for station Entrained and left – destination unknown. ROUEN. Engine broke down 1½ hours	
	29/8/15	7.0 am 8.30 am 10.0 am	BOULOGNE CALAIS ST OMER – detrained – marched 6 miles & billets at RAT DIFFIQUES Laid out a patrol to new defence line (Cd R.7 E 9 mds R.3.) Maj.'s for Poste / C.S. visits the Company	
	6/9/15	6.0 am	marches 18 miles with 69 Bde to SERCUS (billets)	
	7/9/15	8.0 am	" 12 miles " " " to BLEU "	
	8/9/15	8.0 am	" 11 miles to ERQUINGHEM – attached 17th & 6th R's for instruction – v. Batln billets	
	11/9/15	8.0 am	" 11 miles to BAILLEUL – relieved by 125th & 6th R3	
	13/9/15	1.0 pm	Marches back to ERQUINGHEM – night in dugouts	C.B. Boys, Major

Army Form C. 2118.

WAR DIARY
or
INTELLIGENCE SUMMARY.
(Erase heading not required.)

102nd Fd Co. R.E.

Remarks and references to Appendices: **2**

Place	Date	Hour	Summary of Events and Information	Remarks
FROMELLES	15.9.15	—	Handed back to FROMELLES — Took over Billets of 1st Wessex F. Co's and charge of Right sector of line occupied by 23rd Division — from Dead Cow FARM to WATERMEAD. Work allocated — No. 1 Section = SHAFTESBURY AVENUE. (generally) No. 2 " = PARK ROW. No. 3 " = Front Line. No. 4 Section = TRAMWAY AVENUE. H.Q & workshop = ERQUINGHEM (S.S. Line). 69th Brigade (Brig. Gen. Derham) (late Brigade) in our sector. Chief work done — 4 Machine Gun Emplacements front line — 8 Bomb proof Dugouts at H.Qrs Left Battalions — TRAMWAY AVENUE advanced by Infantry brokering Parties.	[C.B.Bury R.E.]
"	by 24.9.15			
"	25.9.15 6. a.m		8th Division on our immediate right attacked & got into enemy trenches. Our Bombardment since 22/9 has been particularly heavy and has knocked enemy trenches about severely. 102 L. C.? still in Billets. 23rd Division standing by but elements of 8th Division reported to have returned from enemy trenches before and after dark.	
"	16.10.15		Sergeant Garner 1 Section — flesh wound by bullet in forearm — 1st Casualty. A/R reinforced of 1 NCO and 2 Saps, 2 Drivers joined Co?	
"	" 17.10.15		Chief work since 24/9 — Owing to alleged mining, support line between BURNT FARM and Dead Cow FARM just in better order and wire strengthened as a Retrenchment. 3 Redoubts — 50 feet diameter Constructed behind Trenches 55-57. TRAMWAY AVENUE advanced. 6 Bombproofs under construction at R.T.B.H.Qr. BOIS GRENIER LINE added to our area to work.	[C.S.B Maj. R.E.]

Army Form C. 2118

(3)

WAR DIARY
or
INTELLIGENCE SUMMARY.
(Erase heading not required.)

Instructions regarding War Diaries and Intelligence Summaries are contained in F. S. Regs., Part II. and the Staff Manual respectively. Title pages will be prepared in manuscript.

Place	Date	Hour	Summary of Events and Information	Remarks and references to Appendices
ERCUINGHEM	24/9	9 p.m	One Searchlight turned on for 3 periods of 10 minutes in French s/b — worked well — did not attract special attention — this was in connection with use of Naval Ammunition (B) gun (?) in DOG LEG road. Note: The Hd. Wr. Section should immediately he provided with a set of Farriers Tools & as well as an ack section. The distance of billets from Comm: Trenches is great (3 miles) and in consequence men in billets were in motor lorries (no many other) and are far distant Communication very difficult and found ones also for H. Q Cars & Unit be invaluable for and more than useful	C.B's manifest
do.	16.10		A/Sergt E. Garner wounded slightly (at duty) — bullet right forearm — private walk.	
	25.10		Nor Sketon lent to 128th to Co. R.E. (2 Lieut. W. Hughes) for work in left sector of Divisional area.	C.R.S. Hayne

23rd Khaïrum

102 w/ F.C.R.E.
Vol 2

121/7654

Nov. 15.

CONFIDENTIAL

War Diary
of
162nd Field Coy R.E.

from 1. XI. 15 to 30. XI. 15

(Volume II.)

WAR DIARY or INTELLIGENCE SUMMARY.

Army Form C. 2118.

102nd Fd. Amb. R.A.M.C. (4)

Place	Date	Hour	Summary of Events and Information	Remarks and references to Appendices
Erquinghem	2/11/15		Nol Section rejoined from attachment to 121st F.A. R.A.M.C. Work normally distributes as follows.— No. 1 Section – with Right Battalion (2 Lt A.W. Hopkins) 2. Section – with Left Battalion (Lieut H.G. Edicoton) 3. Section – Machine Gun emplacements - front line (Lt J.D. Bird) 4. Section – TRAMWAY AVENUE & Redoubts (Lieut D.G. Robb) Workshops & Transport in ERQUINGHEM under Capt H.P.A. Kenneyer, R.E. Drivers organised in A, B, C, D. groups (each of 6 to 8 men) to work times at transport M.O. Over a period of 2 days A+B group do morning and night work and C+D afternoon the 1st day and C+D groups afternoon. the 1st day and morning and night of 2nd day – all drivers then get one night in bed out of two. The supplies home from a small E. gunpit, for permanent daily duties, such as hot ration etc., advance store, water cart, ration etc.	(Erquinghem)
do.	12/11/15		Shelling by enemy has been heavier in our front since 9th instant – a few 5.9" shells have fallen within ¼ mile of our billets, in line of Rue du B162 road. Rain began again in 10th, and drainage of all trenches is becoming a serious problem. The effect of the wet in the old trench pits is very marked, and clearly brings out the following points: (a). Sand bags are useless as a walling material to carry anything – the weight pull the flour. (b). They are of value as a semi-breastwork – that's be filled by turfbone for roof of shelter as a slow fragmentary revetment, higher than 3 courses, all such revetment should be hurdles, wire hurdles or planking, and time given to carefull anchoring backs, will always be repaid. (c). A line of anchor junipers that will not rust would be invaluable.	EBA/Major

Army Form C. 2118.

WAR DIARY
or
INTELLIGENCE SUMMARY.
(Erase heading not required.)

Place	Date	Hour	Summary of Events and Information	Remarks and references to Appendices
ERQUINGHEM	29/XI/15		The following casualties occurred on the dates specified. No 90363 - Pte Nicholson. A - 19.XI.15 - shot through the lungs while standing beside a pair of friends at North end of SHAFTESBURY AVENUE, he was buried at - ERQUINGHEM on 20th Nov. 26.XI.15. No 49060 Capt. Croxen. T.C. (was beaten in the neck through the nick by a sniper while walking behind the BRIDOUX SALIENT, he was buried at ERQUINGHEM on 26.XI.Nov. On 10th Nov orders were issued to concentrate on revetment - I.E. exit of SHAFTESBURY AVENUE. 2 sections have been and 6th are working on this. Wood posts & boarding are used, the posts being anchored to pickets by wire, the wire is pulled through the parapet by means of a "bodkin" 9 ft long with an open eye at the end. The bodkin is 3/4" round iron 9ft long with an open eye at the end. The bodkin is pushed through the parapet till the eye is through, the wire is hooked in and then pulled back so the bodkin is withdrawn. The head of the bodkin is bent up, so as to reduce the friction which would be caused if the whole bodkin were of the same thickness. On 22nd Nov the Right Brigade took over 7 trenches from the 8th Division & handed over 2 trenches to the Left Brigade. The new trenches are in a very rough state compared to the others, parapet low, traverses few, overheads bad or non existent, fire steps in many places non existent.	

Army Form C. 2118.

WAR DIARY
or
INTELLIGENCE SUMMARY.
(Erase heading not required.)

Place	Date	Hour	Summary of Events and Information	Remarks and references to Appendices
			Trenches now under the care of this Company are I.31.1; I.31.2; I.31.3. I.31.4; I.31.5; I.32; I.26.1; I.26.2; I.26.5; I.26.4. Distribution of Sections since being on new Trenches:- No I Section - SHAFTESBURY AVENUE and technical work to the left (B) Battalion. No II Section - SHAFTESBURY AVENUE No III Section - Machine gun emplacements No IV Section - Improving the flooring of QUEER ST and technical work for right (A) Battalion.	
25.11.			On 25th November orders were received that the Company would work under direct orders of CRE and not as before under the G.O.C. Brigade occupying the trenches. 1 Corpl + 1 Driver went on leave to ENGLAND.	
28.11.			C. Coy of 5 SOUTH STAFFORDSHIRE Regt (PIONEERS) were attached for work with this Coy. O.C. both Companies inspected the new line and decided on the work to be done - viz QUEER ST. flooring, revetment and rivving	

A.R.M.
Capt RE

Army Form C. 2118.

WAR DIARY
or
INTELLIGENCE SUMMARY.
(Erase heading not required.)

Place	Date	Hour	Summary of Events and Information	Remarks and references to Appendices
			its parapet. FRONT LINE :- making traverses and raising the front parapet.	MSS. Capt R.

J.D. Abernethy
Capt HRC
O/C 162 Coy R.E.

102 nd FORR.
Vol: 3

16/791

23/w/51

WAR DIARY or INTELLIGENCE SUMMARY

Army Form C. 2118.

102nd Feby 1918

Place	Date	Hour	Summary of Events and Information	Remarks and references to Appendices
Erquinghem	2/12		The following casualties have occurred on 2/12 — No. 63727 L/Cpl Collier, No. 63755 Sapper Bridges, No. 69833 Sapper Vick, No. 33604 Sapper Grount — wounded by a shell in front trenches. Sapper Butler rather seriously.	
	8/12		No. 61044 Sapper Tyler — wounded in ankle by a rifle bullet.	CSM myr
	9/12		Erquinghem — our dug out shelter from 1–3 pm. = about 30 men killed. S.G. Tellos near Church end. Filling churchyard. New efforts to entrenching being made, principally to keep water out in RLWES at BOIS GRENIER and QUEEN ST. and BAY AVENUE are the worst. Sapps of areas — these water in places — work generally is much impeded. The toppes North of ERQUINGHEM bridge i.e. water over it. Causeway North of ERQUINGHEM bridge South.	(PS) myr
Erquinghem	27/12		The 76.25 L.S. (as previously) working in Right Sector of Divisional area. 20th Division occupy area on our right front. XMAS DAY — uneventful — a few shells near East end of ERQUINGHEM — as usual exchange in trenches. Water level in RLWES again high — 6'3" at LONDON BRIDGE, but trenches not so bad as water/ drainage arrangements have improved.	C.B. Broques

Army Form C. 2118.

WAR DIARY
or
INTELLIGENCE SUMMARY.
(Erase heading not required.)

102nd Fd Co. R.E.

Place	Date	Hour	Summary of Events and Information	Remarks and references to Appendices
ERQUINGHEM -LYS.	31.12		Water falling again in Commⁿ trenches. Down to 5'6" at LONDON BRIDGE. Work done during month - flooring and repairs to support line from Watos Farm to trees on left of FLAMENGRIE FARM, and drainage. Organisation in front of LONDON BRIDGE as a defensible post. Drainage and revetment of SHAFTESBURY AVENUE = this revetment of 3"x 3" timber 3' apart backed with 1" boarding and about 7' high. Complete on left side (up) and at corner on right side of BAY AVENUE (trench end) = route 20 Division to finish. Raising of floor boards (nailed down in files) in QUEER STREET and half of 9pr. Gun emplacement continued by 1 section. "B", "C", "C" Co. of E.S. Staff (Pioneers) helping R.E. they are short of tools for skilled work.	(signed) C. Graham Capt 102 Fd Co R.E.

102 W F.C.R.E.
Vol: 4
Tan 716

23rd

Vol 5

WAR DIARY
or
INTELLIGENCE SUMMARY.

Army Form C. 2118.

102nd Feb Coy RE
16

Place	Date	Hour	Summary of Events and Information	Remarks and references to Appendices
ERQUINGHEM	1916 1/1		Hole to walk, whole length of QUEER STREET and BAY AVENUE without water being over gumboots so raised.	C.S.B. major
do	6/1		8 Sappers joined Company as Reinforcements.	C.S.B. major
do	7/1		24th Divn FCs relieved 66th Bgde FCs in Right Sector of Divisional area.	C.S.B. major
do	11/1		Cover stamp № 939 issued to unit = stamp № 2044 destroyed. Decided to concentrate R.E. work on defence work in O.E. Line and push out deep communication trenches for the present.	C.S.B. major
do	16/1		Lieut J.D. Birch RE reported being opened fire 4." "Hello" fires at New 18th Bry Pit. where the 102nd Coy Forward Office lives. He found the place taken, but the shell filled with a very fine comman black powder, apparently to moist from damp to explode. 8th Division relieved 20th Division on our Right (S) on 18/1/16 20/1/16.	C.S.B. major
	23.1. 24.1. A.m.		69th Bde relieved 24th Bde in Right Sector of Divn area on 23.1.16 № 51099 Spr Grahm F. wounded in the head by piece of shell, slight, would have been unhurt had he a steel helmet.	
	31.1.		Work done during the month has been generally - № 1 section making new covered works in rear of support-line - № 2 Section getting support-line into good condition № 3 Section constructing & repairing M.G emplacements.	

Army Form C. 2118.

WAR DIARY
or
INTELLIGENCE SUMMARY.
(Erase heading not required.)

102nd Field Coy. R.E.

Place	Date	Hour	Summary of Events and Information	Remarks and references to Appendices
ERQUINGHEM	31.1.		No 4 Section - improving communications used by 23rd/U. Battalion. 9/5 South Staffords. Pioneers have generally worked. C. Coy with No 4 Section & B Coy with No 2 Section, one platoon of B Coy has worked with No 3 Section for a fortnight. Weather has been generally fine and mild. Roads continue in good condition. 2 draught-horses & one riding horse died suddenly on different dates. 3 men admitted to Hospital during the month on 6.1. 20.1 + 31.1. Health of the Coy continues good. Average daily sick 3.4838. 1 Section 207th Fd Coy R.E. 34th Division attached to the Coy on 26.1.16.	

DR Armorque
Capt RE
OC 102 Fd Coy RE.
31.1.16

WAR DIARY or INTELLIGENCE SUMMARY

Army Form C. 2118.

102nd Fd Co R.E.

Place	Date	Hour	Summary of Events and Information	Remarks and references to Appendices
ERQUINGHEM	6.2	—	MOAT FARM AVENUE floorboarded as far as CULVERT FARM = then goes through Communication to WHITE CITY. This part of work done by "C" Coy of Regiment. Latter part of work done by R.E. Pioneers. BREWERY to HUDSON BAY by floorboarding Communication made by R.E. from 'pieces' of ditto thus avoiding a dangerous piece from WHITE CITY to BREWERY. S¹ Platoon on 9¹ commenced rivet work from LONDON BRIDGE to TRAMWAY and "B" Coy do complete cleaning ditches (right work) connecting branches to support line. TRAMWAY had 2 open breaks from shell & repaired by R.E. during week.	(C.S.M. Sgt R.)
ERQUINGHEM	10.2		Instructions received to hand over to 207 & 210 Coys (already attached to 170th (?) Bde) on instructions received to march to hutments near Rd. county	(C.S.B. Sgt R)
	11.2	11.0 am	Vicinity of Bridge shelled at 11.0 am with about 50 — 5.9" The first 4 fell 2 100 yards from Offices billets across River 2, 50 yards to left of billet - remainder more to S.W. near and in 107" Co's billets at Filatures. rather heavy rain during day.	
	12.2		Very heavy shelling practically all day from front line to RUE DELETTREE = more especially on right half of BRIDOUX SALIENT, where 3 - 400 shells fell within 14hr.	(C.S.B. Sgt R)
	15.2		(12.45 - 2.0 pm)	
	16.2		BRIDOUX Salient heavily shelled again Floorboarding from WHITE CITY to BREWERY and EMMA POST in communication trenches completed = being carried on from latter towards STANBURY POST	
	17.2		Completed work in Rupert Rd Int.	
	18.2		207th Fd Co= R.E. took over Sector	C.B Sgt R

Army Form C. 2118.

WAR DIARY
or
INTELLIGENCE SUMMARY.
(Erase heading not required.)

10D ~ 2 CoRE.

Instructions regarding War Diaries and Intelligence Summaries are contained in F. S. Regs., Part II. and the Staff Manual respectively. Title pages will be prepared in manuscript.

Place	Date	Hour	Summary of Events and Information	Remarks and references to Appendices
ERQUINGHEM	22/2	9.am	Marched out to VIEUX BERQUIN - & billeted. 9 - 1 hour punt. Day. Strength of Company. Officers. N.C.Os.	
VIEUX BERQUIN	23/2	9.15 am	Marched to STEENBECQUE - & billeted. 9-30 - 1.30.pm. Snow fell during morning & day about 2" deep - hard frost	(Sig 3 mag sh)
STEENBECQUE	23/2		Recd. orders to move to ESTAIRES on 24/2. Same afternoon - move postponed. Hard frost - snow. 128 OR. G3 marches out to ESTAIRES.	
"	24/2		Drill - frost	
"	25/2	1.30 pm	orders to move to ESTAIRES on 26/2	
		8.30 pm	Move again postponed. Drill - frost. more snow.	(SSA mayor)
"	26/2		Drill - frost.	
"	27/2		Regt. snowing. Thaw began towards 2.Lt. R. Burwell joined unit - midnight.	
"	28/2	5.0 pm	Orders to move with Division on 29/2 with C.B. Bentham tok over a/Butler of C.R.E. Captain A.R.S. Jenner left unit to Command 75 F. Co. R.E.	(Sig M mag sh)
"	29/2	8.0	Dismounted men proceeded by train to BRUAY areas. to join 4th Corps.	
		9.0	Mounted detachment proceeds by march-route to billets Actually billeted at CAMBLAIN-CHATELAIN.	

Army Form C. 2118.

WAR DIARY
or
INTELLIGENCE SUMMARY. 102nd Fd Co RE

(Erase heading not required.)

March 1916

(14)

Place	Date	Hour	Summary of Events and Information	Remarks and references to Appendices
CAMBLAIN CHATELAIN	1/3		Company drill	DWR LXRE
	2/3		Drill — rifle exercises etc	
	3/3		Drill — Snow	
	4/3		Short route march to the Co. drill. Corps General continues to inspect of the 23rd Division at BRUAY	DWR LXRE
	5/3		New pattern gas helmets issued to Co.	
	6/3		Drill	DWR GRE
	7/3	11am	2nd Lt A.M. Cain joined Co. Lt H.G. Easton took up duties as adjutant R.E. Coy. marched out of billets at CAMBLAIN CHATELAIN to ABLAIN-ST-NAZAIRE	
	7/3	1pm	HQs of the Coy remain at GOUY-LES-SERVINS, snow. O.C. watches where Coy settling in cellars, dug outs etc Taking over stores from the French.	
ABLAIN-ST NAZAIRE	8/3		Fixing up cellars etc, pumps, supplies etc. C.R.E. received from leave	DWR GRE
	9/3		Major C.P. Pavenson inspects Co.	

Jy Rob
O.C. 102nd Fd Co RE

Army Form C. 2118.

WAR DIARY
or
INTELLIGENCE SUMMARY. 102nd to C RE
(Erase heading not required.)

March 1916

Instructions regarding War Diaries and Intelligence Summaries are contained in F. S. Regs., Part II and the Staff Manual respectively. Title pages will be prepared in manuscript.

Place	Date	Hour	Summary of Events and Information	Remarks and references to Appendices
ADMN ST NAZAIRE	10.3		Night work in Trenches. 46th Div taking over from French on our Right (Trenches - road line - new Cantonments & inconceivably muddy) ditto.	
	11.3		2 Sections (ditto).	
	12.3		No. 2 & 3 Sections by Route March to RUITZ	
	13.3		Relieved by 2 Section 1/3 LONDON F.C.RE (47th Div). Weather turned warm.	
	14.3		No 1 & 4 Section with Coy by Route March to RUITZ — relieved by remainder 1/3 London F.C.RE	Cathage
RUITZ	15.3		Rest - cleaning up.	
	16.3		Marched 6.30 pm to front line - Came to Sims en Gohelle (7 miles) Reported to OC 5th F.C. RL	Cathage
FOSSE 10	17.3		2 Sections working in BATOLLE line - reconnoitering	Cathage
	18.3		- ditto -	
	19.3		2 Sections - working - do.	
	20.3		2 Sections working BATOLLE line — night work. 1 Section working on over Town for Cutanian O.P. — continuous work 1 Section working on advanced Brown Station — day work	D.T.R. F.C.RE
	21.3		as for 20th	D.T.R. F.C.RE
	22.3		ditto	

Major Barton O.C. 102nd F.W.C. RE taken over duties as CRE, CRE vice Lt Col ......

Army Form C. 2118.

WAR DIARY
or
INTELLIGENCE SUMMARY.
(Erase heading not required.)

Instructions regarding War Diaries and Intelligence Summaries are contained in F. S. Regs., Part II. and the Staff Manual respectively. Title pages will be prepared in manuscript. March 1916

102 Fld. Co. R.E.

Place	Date	Hour	Summary of Events and Information	Remarks and references to Appendices
FOSSE 10	23/3		2 Sections working on BATOLLE line	D.H.R.
			1 Section " O.P.'s, one for French Division, one for our own division.	L.T.R.E.
			½ Section " Advanced Dressing Station	
			Tr. Comr. on SPINNEY ALLEY inspection. Present on very heavy rain. Inspection postponed to start work on this trench; cleaning out, approved to follow on material front.	D.H.R. L.T.R.E.
	24/3		Sections working as on 23rd	
	25/3		— do —	
	26/3		1st Division on the left of our front. 47th Division on the right.	D.H.R. G.R.E.
			2 Sections working on BATOLLE line winning	
			1 Section working on O.P. for our division, which includes station.	
			½ Section on Advanced Dressing Station	
			½ Section working on SPINNEY ALLEY trench	
	27/3		work as on 26th. C.R.E. returns to Head quarters	D.H.R. L.T.R.E.
			Major Bonham acting C.R.E. returns to unit.	D.H.R.

Army Form C. 2118.

17

WAR DIARY
or
INTELLIGENCE SUMMARY.
(Erase heading not required.)

March 1916   102nd Feb. RR

Place	Date	Hour	Summary of Events and Information	Remarks and references to Appendices
Fosse X	28/3	—	Work as 26/3	
"	29/3		ditto — except No 3 section for duty in Fosse X	
"	30/3		ditto — ditto	
"	31/3		ditto — ditto	
			Fosse X shelled from 11.10 am — 1.0 pm by 32 — 8·2" (Naval) shells within enclosure; S Yates touched by a splinter. No damage to horses stables or ramp. Jun Fosse entrance; shooting was very accurate. 40 Officers Men 40 yds. Weather bright & clear	(sd) signed

(B. Boutroue)
Major
O.C. 102nd Feb. RR

Army Form C. 2118.

Vol 7

WAR DIARY
or
INTELLIGENCE SUMMARY.
(Erase heading not required.)

102nd Tol R2

Instructions regarding War Diaries and Intelligence Summaries are contained in F. S. Regs., Part II. and the Staff Manual respectively. Title pages will be prepared in manuscript.

Place	Date	Hour	Summary of Events and Information	Remarks and references to Appendices
Trench Petit Saire	1.4 to 12.4		Work as 29/3. Progress. BATTLE LINE Excavation in new Sector (ANGRES) approaching completion. About half wiring done from North to South. Floor trestling and revetting nearly finished. 13 Traps (= 130 yds) from South. SPINNEY TRENCH clearing through 2 cavities. Obstructed in Traps 71. - up to 20 floored, and clearing CTIRD LINE IN TSOUR CRATER being refused.	(Ashingten) CSsmyth CSsmyth
"	13.4		No 4 Section took over duties at Annex.	
"	16.4		5th Infantry Brigade took over ANGRES SECTION from 6th F.A.E.s put relief of 2nd Division by 2 Divisions.	
"	20.4		No 3 Section (Lieut J.D.Bird) details to work with 13th Machine Gun Section Company on machine gun emplacement and dugouts. The 2nd Sapping Company (formed of one platoon from each Regiment of Brigade) to work with R.E. Field Coy. 3 Platoons but "BAJOLE line and 1 platoon on Trench Sap 6. O.C. is Captain Ranson Oxf + Bucks. Continued rain between 17th & 20th has rendered excavation very difficult, the sand considerably, the sides adhere to spades; communication trenches have suffered fall in slide in badly; neither C.Ts with high boards, while Trench round BULLY CRATERS badly damaged by shell fire between 2-3 pm 21st, but Infantry practically cleared it by 3.0 a.m.; chiefly a nine fullers between posts.	(C.S.Smyth)
"	21.4 to 22.4	—	Milder. No 4 Section [2] Lieut R Burnell) proceeds with men to the attaches to 1/4 Landon Field at ASLAIN ST. NAZARRE (17/4.4.R). Very wet	(B Bhupuch)

Army Form C. 2118.

WAR DIARY
or
INTELLIGENCE SUMMARY.

(Erase heading not required.)

102nd (Field) Co. RE

1916

19

Instructions regarding War Diaries and Intelligence Summaries are contained in F. S. Regs., Part II. and the Staff Manual respectively. Title pages will be prepared in manuscript.

Place	Date	Hour	Summary of Events and Information	Remarks and references to Appendices
Foss X. Sains-	23.4		Nos 2 & 3 Sections moved to forward billets in BULLY.	P.B.Bhqrs.
	24.4		Major Bonham ordered to RUTZ to officiate as C.R.E. 23rd Division	DYR LTRE
	25.4		Hour in progress on OP FOSSE X, BULLY CRATERS, BATONS hill and	
	26.4		various MG Emplacements in Dugouts	DYR LTCE
	27.4		working with 5th Inf Brigade, 2nd Division.	
	28.4			
	29.4		Return came from CRE to move to RUTZ in 3 days.	DYR
	30.4		2 Sections of East Anglian Field Co RE (T) to carry on Part of work	LTRE
	30.4		with the Coy is at RUTZ. Handed over to Major Ireson O.C.	
			E A Fld Co RE.	
			D. Roth. Lt RE	
			O.C. 102nd Field Co RE	

WAR DIARY
or
INTELLIGENCE SUMMARY.
(Erase heading not required.)

Army Form C. 2118.

1516   102 Field Co. R.E.   20 Vol 8

XXIII

Place	Date	Hour	Summary of Events and Information	Remarks and references to Appendices
RUITZ	1.5		H.Q. and 1 Section, Transport marched out of FOSSE X to RUITZ (for winter rest). Rear FOSSE X 3.30 p.m. arrive RUITZ 5.30 p.m.	D.R.
			2 Sections marched out of BULLY at 7 p.m. arrive RUITZ 10.15 p.m. 1 Section marched out of VILLERS-AU-BOIS, 3.30 p.m. arrive RUITZ 7 p.m.	D.R.
"	2.5		1 Section leaves unit (temporarily) to proceed to PERNES to carry out work at	
			The Corps School of Instruction, relieving 1 section of the 101st Fd Co R.E. 2 Sections working at HOUDAIN section huts for storing shells, etc. (one of these section remains at HOUDAIN, living in huts)	D.R.
"	3.5		2 Sections working on huts one at HOUDAIN and one at BRUAY 1 Section permitting extensive weapon tra	D.R.
"	4.5		as on 3rd	
	5.5			
	6.5	3.30 p.m.	H.Q., Transport, & 3 Sections inspected by Divisional General (Major General Barrington)	D.R.
	7.5		2 Sections working HOUDAIN & BRUAY. 1 Section at PERNES.	D.R.
	8.5		1 Section resuming a touring weapons	D.R.
	9.6	3.30	H.Q. Transport, + 2 Sections marched out of RUITZ to FOSSE X. one section remaining behind at HOUDAIN, and one at PERNES	D.R.

Army Form C. 2118.

WAR DIARY
or
INTELLIGENCE SUMMARY.

(Erase heading not required.)   102nd Field Co RE.   1916   (21)

Instructions regarding War Diaries and Intelligence Summaries are contained in F. S. Regs., Part II. and the Staff Manual respectively. Title pages will be prepared in manuscript.

Place	Date	Hour	Summary of Events and Information	Remarks and references to Appendices
FOSSE X	10.5		Cleaning up materials etc and amongst home lines. 1 Section sent to relieve 1st in AIX	DUR.
SAINS-EN-GOHELLE	11.5		# Section from PERNES rejoins the Co. Section at HOUDAIN, Trup. attached 2nd Division. Tel. the work that is completed. Work proceeds in various parts of the line — BATOLLE, PYRENEES etc. M.G. Emplacements & dugouts. Coy being attached for work to the 69th Bgde.	DUR.
	12.5		2½ Sections at work in the line as above, and ½ Section outin [?]	
	13.5			
	14.5			DUR
	16.5			
	17.5			
	18.5		2 Sections sent to relieve in BULLY (one from FOSSE X, & one from AIX) Coy (less 1 Section at HOUDAIN, Transport) move to relieve in BULLY.	
BULLY	19.5		Work consists of lining BATOLLE Line, similar PYRENEES Tunnel, M.G. Emplacements and dugouts, some in front line & some in reserve line	
	20.5		1st Division, 1st Bgde on our right, and 47th Division on our left. Heavy bombardment all afternoon, earthquake shocks on 50 ft. Gas reports to hand but nothing felt in BULLY	DUR
	21.5		2 generals [?] via relief arrangements, went	

#353   Wt. W2544/1454   700,000   5/15   D. D. & L.   A.D.S.S./Forms/C. 2118.

Army Form C. 2118.

WAR DIARY
or
INTELLIGENCE SUMMARY.

(Erase heading not required.)

102nd Field Co RE.

1916

22

Instructions regarding War Diaries and Intelligence Summaries are contained in F. S. Regs., Part II. and the Staff Manual respectively. Title pages will be prepared in manuscript.

Place	Date	Hour	Summary of Events and Information	Remarks and references to Appendices
BULLY	22.5		Work as usual. Bombardment less heavy than afternoon of 21.5 during the afternoon. Wind changed round, protecting us from German wire impressions.	D.R.
	23.5		Section reports sent, having completed its work for the Corps at HOUDAIN with connection of work on windings for heavy ammunition.	D.R.
	24.5		Sections working as usual. 3½" in dump, on ½ Section been detailed at FOSSE X preparing for return to Infantry, attached to Lancashire Fusiliers (attached). Huns counter attacked FOSSE 8 mines but were kept a long way off and fighting continues.	D.R.
	25.5 26.5	}D.R.	as on 24th.	D.R.
	27.5		Work as on 24th. S.O.S. received at 11 P.M. from D.1, D. canceled on being taken.	
	5.30	on 28th		
	26.6		Work continued, huns most active evening FOSSE X.	D.R.
			The road near COUPIGNY (FOSSE X) SAINS-EN-GOHELLE has been shelled the last two or three days (Heavy HE) about D.2 Co. Headquarters.	

#353 Wt. W2544/1454 700,000 5/15 D. D. & L. A.D.S.S./Forms/C. 2118.

Army Form C. 2118.

WAR DIARY
or
INTELLIGENCE SUMMARY.

(Erase heading not required) 102nd Field Co. R.E. 1916

Instructions regarding War Diaries and Intelligence Summaries are contained in F. S. Regs., Part II. and the Staff Manual respectively. Title pages will be prepared in manuscript.

No. 23

Place	Date	Hour	Summary of Events and Information	Remarks and references to Appendices
BULLY	30.5		24th Infantry Regt & (Bag. Genrle OXEY) reliens 65th Infantry Regt (Bag. Genrle LAUNOY). 102nd (Fld) Co. R.E. attached 24th Regts for work. No infantry appear to be at work. Have a frontage of about 80 metres. Have no data as to the trenches, dug-outs, wire, etc on same as usual. Enquiries will begin tomorrow.	DR
	31.5		Subordinates completing known information. Dug-outs are now the chief need. One 15' deep, one 10' deep, in reserve trench wanted. The noise of hand charges, which means a bomb job, is not to hand. Existing weather good for the establishment of same.	DR

Dy Roll. Lt. R.E.
a.o.c. 102nd Field Co. R.E.

Army Form C. 2118.

WAR DIARY
or
INTELLIGENCE SUMMARY.
(Erase heading not required.)

102nd Field Co. RE

June 1916

Vol. 9 (24)

Instructions regarding War Diaries and Intelligence Summaries are contained in F. S. Regs., Part II. and the Staff Manual respectively. Title pages will be prepared in manuscript.

Place	Date	Hour	Summary of Events and Information	Remarks and references to Appendices
BULLY	1.6		Offr for work to 24th Inf Brigade (Sgn Oxley) Work in progress deep dugouts construction & wire support lines. 1st Division on our left, 2nd Division on our right.	D.R.
	2.6		Co on I.G.	D.R.
	3.6		Lt Col Bannon (C.R.E) takes over from river drains (S.6). Major Baulan (a C.R.E) leaves for England on leave.	D.R.
	4.6		Co on I.G.	D.R.
	5.6		1 Section (Lieut Nixon), 1st Field Co R.E. R.N. Division attached to the Co for instruction.	D.R.
	6.6		Section R.E.R.N. spent up to work with us for instruction.	D.R.
	7.6		C.E. VII Corps (Brig. Gen. Kenyon), C R E Capt Gnatham (S.O. 47th Div) and my 6 Inspect Corps work in trenches, representing deep dugouts.	D.R.
	8.6		Reviews orders to be in readiness to Entrain. Orders - more into billets at Lapugnoy.	D.R.
	9.6		Co to Lapugnoy.	
	10.6		Co on rest. Parties endeavour.	D.R.
	11.6		Recce parties for 1 Section to proceed to LA THIEULOYE with the section from 4 London R.E. (T.F.) 47th Division in view of further	D.R.

WAR DIARY or INTELLIGENCE SUMMARY

Army Form C. 2118.

102 Field Co. R.E. — 25

1916

Place	Date	Hour	Summary of Events and Information	Remarks and references to Appendices
BULLY	11.6		1 Section of 4th London Co RE (T.F.) 47th Division came to Bouvigny wets in Bully. 1 Section (21st Divnl) 102 Field Co RE proceed to LATHIEULOYE to attach for work (from 4th London)	D4R
	12.6	p.m. 4.30	Have now under the 1st 4th London Co RE (majority) O.C. marches out of Bully to AUCHY and places in HERSIN. CARLIN, MAISNIL - RUITZ, RANCHICOURT, LA COMTÉ (Batt Hd Qrs) to LA THIEULOYE (arrive 10.15 pm)	D4R
LA THIEULOYE	13.6 14.6		4th Divn (T.F.) relieving 23rd Divn on this front. Camp Fatigues	D4R
	15.6	a.m 9.30	Marches from west LA THIEULOYE to billets VERCHIN. CAPT J.F. OUCHTERLONY assumed command of the Coy.	D4R
VERCHIN	16.6	a.m. 10.30	Marched from billets VERCHIN to billets MATRINGHEM	p.
MATRINGHEM	17.6		Instruction in use of Weldon Trestle	p.
	18.6		Church parade and Company fatigues	p.
	19.6		Divisional field day	p.
	20.6		Instruction in pontooning and Weldon Trestle	p.
	21.6 22.6		Infantry Training	p.

Army Form C. 2118.

WAR DIARY
or
INTELLIGENCE SUMMARY.
(Erase heading not required.)

102 Field Company RE

1916

(26)

Instructions regarding War Diaries and Intelligence Summaries are contained in F. S. Regs., Part II. and the Staff Manual respectively. Title pages will be prepared in manuscript.

Place	Date	Hour	Summary of Events and Information	Remarks and references to Appendices
MATRINGHEM	23.6		Inspection by O.R.E. - Packing wagons for entrainment.	
	24.6	P.M. 2.30	Marched out, wrong BERGUETTE Station 9.40 p.m. Pontoon wagons followed 3 hours later	
BERGUETTE Station	25.6	A.M. 12.40	Left by train for new area.	
LONGUEAU	25.6	A.M. 8.0	Arrived LONGUEAU and detrained. Marched to billets at YSEUX.	
YSEUX	26.6		Company fatigues	
	27.6		Company training	
	28.6	P.M. 2.15	Preparing to march to new billets. Received orders to remain in present billets till further orders.	
	29.6		Infantry drill and physical exercises	
	30.6	A.M. 10.45	Received orders to march to ALLONVILLE.	
		12.0	Marched out from YSEUX.	
		P.M. 6.45	Arrived at ALLONVILLE.	

JP Duckworth
Capt. RE
O.C. 102nd Field Coy RE.

23/July

102 F.R.E
Vol 10

Confidential

War Diary
of
102nd Field Cy. R.E.

from 1st July 1916 to 31st July 1916

Army Form C. 2118.

WAR DIARY
or
INTELLIGENCE SUMMARY.
(Erase heading not required.)

102nd Field Company R.E. (27)

1916

Place	Date	Hour	Summary of Events and Information	Remarks and references to Appendices
ALLONVILLE	1.7	A.M. 11.0	Received orders to be ready to move at 6 hour's notice	/o
		P.M. 8.45	Received orders to proceed at once to MORAMU LA HOUSSOYE	/o
		10.15	Marched out of ALLONVILLE	
	2.7	A.M.	Arrived at LA HOUSSOYE & went into billets	/o /o
LA HOUSSOYE	2.7	1.0 P.M. 6.0	Received orders to march at 9.15 p.m. to BAIZIEUX - HENENCOURT.	/o /o
	3.7	9.0 A.M.	Arrived at HENENCOURT & went into billets	/o
		1.0	" " " "	/o
HENENCOURT	4.7	A.M. 1.0	Received orders to march to DERNANCOURT	/o
		NOON 9.30	Marched from HENENCOURT	/o
		12.0	Arrived at DERNANCOURT and bivouacked.	/o
DERNANCOURT		P.M. 6.0	Ordered by C.R.E. to take company to BÉCOURT Chateau for work on strong points under 89th Brigade.	/o
		7.0	Marched up to top of hill short of BÉCOURT wood & awaited instructions	/o
		10.0	Informed by C.R.E. that company was not required to returned to camp	/o
	5.7		Instructed by C.R.E. to reconnoitre new communication trenches in X 20 D and X 26 B South at LA-BOISELLE. Took Lieut. HUGHES with me to see the former.	/o

Army Form C. 2118.

28

WAR DIARY
or
INTELLIGENCE SUMMARY.
(Erase heading not required.)

102nd Field Company R.E.   1916

Instructions regarding War Diaries and Intelligence Summaries are contained in F. S. Regs., Part II. and the Staff Manual respectively. Title pages will be prepared in manuscript.

Place	Date	Hour	Summary of Events and Information	Remarks and references to Appendices
DERNANCOURT	5.7		2nd Lieut BURWELL to the latter both requiring a lot of work. The Company paraded at 5.30 p.m. for work Recce. Nos 1 + 2 Sections with one company of pioneers to work on Northern Trench, nos 4 + part of No 3 (Coln in trenches). 14 men of No. 3 Section took over maintenance of tramway. Sgt Carr and 2 men the USNA pumping station.	
	6.7		Owing to heavy shelling party were unable to reach Northern trench 100' of Southern Trench was cleaned out, widened to 3'3" and deepened to 4'9". Two section parties at 5.30 p.m went on Southern Trench.	DuR
	7.7	3.0 a.m.	Trench washed up and made passable. Lieut D.C. ROSS took over command of the Co. temporarily, the O.C. Capt COCHTERLONY taking charge of the 101st + 128th Fuseliers on the operations (Until O.C's taking over arrived in action the pioneer day. 1 Section (2nd Lieut ATT (ROWE)) pioneers for work, road repair, to REDOUBT.	DuR
		7pm		DuR
	8.7.16	Noon	1 Section (2nd Lieut ATT (Clarke)) pioneers for work upon ST REDOUBT. Lieut T.D. Ball sent out to reconnoitre new tram from REDOUBT Chateau to LOZENGE wood.	DuR

WAR DIARY or INTELLIGENCE SUMMARY

Army Form C. 2118.

1916 **102nd Field Co. RE.** (29)

Place	Date	Hour	Summary of Events and Information	Remarks and references to Appendices
BERNAN COURT	27/9/15	9.15 a.m.	Two sections (2 Lts. BURNELL & TYSSEN) proceeded from BEAUCOURT to LOZENGE wood, turned on road from BEAUCOURT to LOZENGE wood, arrived on the 6 P.m. 1/2 Section arrived to report to O.C. 10th Rations at 7 P.m. at LOZENGE wood, and to remained there till 12.30 a.m. (10/7) when they obtained horses. 2 P.m. Capt OUGHTERLONY commenced 1 Coy	DHR
	10/7	8 am	2 Sections proceed to work on road repair, road from BEAUCOURT to LOZENGE wood until the 2 P.m. 1 Section proceeds 5 P.m. for road repair near BEAUCOURT station about 3 P.m. orders for work of 23rd Div. by 1st Div. received.	DHR
	11/7	—	Work as yesterday.	
	12/7	AM 8.45	Orders received for 2 sections to proceed at once to CONT ALMAISON for work on consolidation. Arrived there at 11.45 am. Worked on strong point, preparing gun positions & M.G. emplacements & clearing ELLIO hill 6.30 p.m. Excellent progress made in conjunction with the 101st & 128th field companies who	JD

Army Form C. 2118.

WAR DIARY
or
INTELLIGENCE SUMMARY.
(Erase heading not required.)

102nd Field Company R.E. 1916   30

Place	Date	Hour	Summary of Events and Information	Remarks and references to Appendices
DERAN- COURT	11/7 (contd)		Nine miles marching. Men thought in all were fairly stuffed & sufficient purposes was made to render them useful. No casualties	/o
	12/7	A.M. 11.25	Marched on to 26th Field Company, 1st Division, and handed over	/o
		P.M. 3.25	Arrival at FRECHENCOURT & went into billets	/o
FRECHEN- -COURT	13/7	A.M. 7.20	Orders received to move to MORLIERS-AU-BOIS	/o
		10.45	Above orders cancelled. Company ordered to stand fast in present billets. Company fatigues, cleaning & repairing wagons etc	/o
	14/7 to 20/7		Making preparations under orders of C.E. II Corps.	/o
	20/7	6.10 P.M.	Received orders to proceed tomorrow to MILLENCOURT starting at 8 A.M.	/o
	21/7	A.M. 8.0	Marched out of FRECHENCOURT.	
MILLENCOURT		11.0	Arrival at MILLENCOURT - Mounted and No. 4 Section into billets remainder into tents. Lecture on gas shells in the afternoon and inspection of tube helmets & goggles.	/o
	22/7	A.M. 11.0	Received total order from C.R.E. to be ready to move at half an hour notice from midnight 22/23.	/o
	23/7 - 25/7		Company Training. No. 2 Section on 24th & 25th preparing drainage scheme for camp in HENENCOURT wood	/o
	25/7	P.M. 2.30	No. 4 Section left to proceed to DERNANCOURT to take over from 26th Field Co. 1st Division	/o

Army Form C. 2118.

WAR DIARY
or
INTELLIGENCE SUMMARY.
(Erase heading not required.)

102nd Field Company R.E.   1916   (31)

Instructions regarding War Diaries and Intelligence Summaries are contained in F. S. Regs., Part II. and the Staff Manual respectively. Title pages will be prepared in manuscript.

Place	Date	Hour	Summary of Events and Information	Remarks and references to Appendices
MILLENCOURT	26/7	9.0 AM	Marched out to DERNANCOURT arriving latter place 10.30 AM. Took over camp from 26th Field Company 11th Division.	/o
	27/7/18		No. 2 section repaired road from CONTALMAISON to CONTALMAISON VILLA by night, leaving it open to traffic throughout.	
BÉCOURT WOOD	27/7		Company moved to BÉCOURT WOOD taking over bivouacks from 26th Field Coy. I made reconnaissance of strong points at the CUTTING and CONTALMAISON VILLA. No. 1 Section worked on latter point by night, deepening the fire trenches & making open M.G. emplacements into severely interfered with by shellfire. One and a half sections working on strong point at the CUTTING. One section	
	28/7		worked half a day on strong point at CONTALMAISON VILLA. One section alternative road from FRICOURT to CONTALMAISON via SHELTER WOOD. One Section wiring CONTALMAISON VILLA keep by night. Sapper CADDOW slightly wounded.	/o
	29/7		One section on strong point at the CUTTING. Two sections on alternative road from FRICOURT to CONTALMAISON. One section wiring keep at CONTALMAISON VILLA by night. A/Serjt. BURNETT wounded.	/o
	30/7		One section on strong point at the CUTTING, and one at CONTALMAISON villa. One section on road repairs & making of alternative road to CONTALMAISON.	/o

WAR DIARY
or
INTELLIGENCE SUMMARY

Army Form C. 2118.

102nd Field Company R.E.   1916   (32)

Place	Date	Hour	Summary of Events and Information	Remarks and references to Appendices
BECOURT WOOD	30/7		Sapper RIVETT slightly wounded, but remains at duty. Lieut H.V. HUGHES struck off strength of company on transfer to Headquarters III Corps as assistant staff officer to the Chief Engineer.	
	31/7		Two sections (Lieut BIRD and 2/Lieut TYSSEN) on CONTALMAISON VILLA KEEP. One section (2/Lieut BURNELL) on THE CUTTING KEEP. One section (2/Lieut CLARKE) on road repairs. Sapper GARRETT wounded in CRE's office.	

J.P. Mulholland
Capt RE
OC 102nd Field Company RE.

23rd Divisional Engineers

102nd FIELD COMPANYR. E.

AUGUST 1 9 1 6

Vol 11

War Diary of

102nd (Field) Company R.E.

from

1st August 1916 to 31st August 1916

Army Form C. 2118.

WAR DIARY
or
INTELLIGENCE SUMMARY — 102nd Field Company RE

(Erase heading not required.)

Place	Date	Hour	Summary of Events and Information	Remarks and references to Appendices
BECOURT WOOD	1/8		Nos 1 & 3 Section (Lieut BIRD and 2/Lieut TYSSEN) on CONTALMAISON VILLA KEEP. No 2 Section (2/Lieut BURNELL) on THE CUTTING KEEP. No 2 section (2/Lieut CLARKE) on road repairs. Sapper BENNETT wounded in action. " JACKSON F. " " " " remains at duty. " COOPER " " " " (shell shock).	/o /o
	2/8		Work as for 1st inst. Sapper HARRIS W. wounded in action	
	3/8		No 1 section (2/Lieut TYSSEN) on CONTALMAISON VILLA KEEP. No 4 " (2/Lieut BURNELL) on THE CUTTING KEEP	/o
	4/8		Nos 2 & 3 section (2/Lieut CLARKE and LIEUT. BIRD) commenced work on Crucifix redoubt in BLACK WATCH ALLEY.	/o
	5/8		" " " " " . Wiring of BLACK WATCH ALLEY KEEP started Sapper CHAMBERS wounded in action, remains at duty	/o
	6/8		Work as for 3rd inst.	/o /o/

Army Form C. 2118.

WAR DIARY
or
INTELLIGENCE SUMMARY.
(Erase heading not required.)

102nd Field Company RE (34)

1916

Place	Date	Hour	Summary of Events and Information	Remarks and references to Appendices
BECOURT WOOD	6/8		Explained details of work in hand etc, to O.C. 91st Field Coy. R.E. Sapper GADD slightly wounded but remains at duty.	
		P.M. 4.0	Received orders to hand over to O.C. 91st Field Coy R.E. 15th Division on 8th inst. and march to BEHENCOURT.	/o
	7/8		Handing over to 91st Field Coy. - Digging shelter trenches near Kinoraike	/o
	8/9		Completed handing over to 91st Field Coy R.E. marched out from BECOURT wood	/o
BEHENCOURT	9/8	A.M. 8.30 P.M. 2.0	Arrival at BEHENCOURT & went into billets. Company fatigues. Advanced party (2/Lieut. TYSSEN and 2 O.R.) left MERICOURT station at 4.0 p.m. for Xth Corps area.	/o
	10/8	A.M. 6.0	Advanced party (2/Lieut. CLARKE and 2 O.R.) left MERICOURT station for Xth Corps area.	/o
		P.M. 2.30	Transport and cyclists under Capt. ROBB marched out en route to Xth Corps area via POULAINVILLE.	/o
	11/8	P.M. 2.30 5.0	Marched out from BEHENCOURT. Left FRECHENCOURT by rail arriving LONGPRÉ (N. ABBEVILLE) at 9.30 p.m.	/o

Army Form C. 2118.

WAR DIARY
INTELLIGENCE SUMMARY. 102nd Field Company R.E.

Instructions regarding War Diaries and Intelligence Summaries are contained in F.S. Regs., Part II and the Staff Manual respectively. Title pages will be prepared in manuscript.

(Erase heading not required.)

1916

35

Place	Date	Hour	Summary of Events and Information	Remarks and references to Appendices
FAMECHON	12/8	A.M. 1.0	Arrived by road from LONG PRE station, rejoining transport.	/o
	13/8	P.M. 1.0	Marched out to entrain at LONG PRE station	/o
LONGPRÉ		6.41	Train left LONGPRÉ	/o
BAILLEUL	14/8	A.M. 3.50	Arrived at BAILLEUL, detrained and marched to billets near FLETRE arriving 8.0 A.M.	/o
FLETRE	15/8		Rifle + gas helmet inspection — company fatigues. Proceeded to DOUDOU FARM to take over work site from 237th Field Company, 41st Division	/o
	16/8	A.M. 7.0	Company marched out, arriving DOUDOU FARM at 11.45 A.M. Took section Officers round the line in the evening	/o
DOUDOU FARM	17/8 — 23/8		Works distribution — Nos 1, 2, + 3 sections in Left, Centre, + Right sections at CENTRE sector of Divisional Front (Trenches 103-120 inclusive). No 4 Section in reserve - workshops, dumps etc.	/o
	22/8	A.M. 1.0	Lance Cpl. PLOWMAN killed, when in charge of infantry wiring party 2/Lieut. TYSSEN admitted to hospital	/o
	24/8		No 1 section withdrawn from line, being relieved by No 4 Section	/o
	25/8		2/Lieut. CLARKE wounded by rifle grenade, + admitted to hospital	/o
	31/8		No 2 section withdrawn from line, being relieved by No 1 Section Lance Cpl. CHAMBERS wounded by rifle grenade.	/o

J.P. MCWhirter Capt RE
O.C. 102nd Field Coy RE

vol 12

2b

Confidential

War Diary of
102nd Fd Coy R.E
from
Sept 1st 1916 to Sept 30th 1916

Army Form C. 2118.

WAR DIARY
or
INTELLIGENCE SUMMARY
102nd Field Company R.E.

(Erase heading not required.)

1916.

Place	Date	Hour	Summary of Events and Information	Remarks and references to Appendices
DOUDOU FARM	1/9 - 2/9		Nos 3, 1 & 4 sections in Right, Centre & left sectors of company front respecting	
	2/9	P.M. 5.0	No. 2 Section in reserve, workshops, duty etc. Received orders to hand over to 81st Field Company R.E. tomorrow & march to FLETRE	/o /o
	3/9	P.M. 10.15	2nd Lieut. Clarke rejoined from hospital. Company marched out. I remained behind, handed over ink and blocks to 81st Field Company R.E. & took the C.O. & another officer round the line. I rejoined the company. Inspection of kit, rifles, gas helmets and company equipment.	/o
FLETRE	4/9	P.M. 9.30	Received orders to entrain on the 5th for new area, transport to go by road.	/o
	5/9	A.M. 7.0	Advance party of 1 officer and 2 O.R. handed as ordered and waited till 10.0 A.M. for the lorry.	
		A.M. 10.0	Water cart, cooks cart and mess cart, under 2/Lieut. CLARKE handed out for entrainment at BAILLEUL	
		10.45	Dismounted portion of company marched out, entrained at BAILLEUL, leaving at 14.28 P.M. and arriving ST OMER at 6.0 P.M.	

36

Army Form C. 2118.

WAR DIARY
or
INTELLIGENCE SUMMARY
(Erase heading not required.)

102nd Field Company R.E. (37)

1916

Place	Date	Hour	Summary of Events and Information	Remarks and references to Appendices
FLÊTRE	5/9	A.M. 11.30	Transport and cyclists under Capt. Ross marched out.	
BASSE -BOULOGNE		P.M. 9.0	Dismounted personnel arrived at new billets	
	6/9	11.15 P.M.	Transport proceeding by rail to WIZERNES arrived at new billets	/b
	7/9 – 9/9	4.0 P.M.	Overhauling company equipment, repairing road, sharpening tools, washing and painting wagons.	/b
	8/9		Advanced party of 2 O.R. left for AMIENS	/b
	10/9	A.M. 11.0	Transport and cyclists marched out to entrainment at ARQUES	
		P.M. 12.15	Dismounted personnel — " —	
ARQUES		5.39	left by train for SALEUX.	
SALEUX	11/9	A.M. 2.0	Arrived and detrained at SALEUX	/b
ALLONVILLE	12/9	8.0 A.M. 9.0	Arrived at ALLONVILLE and went into billets	/b
		P.M. 2.0	marched out of ALLONVILLE	/b
		7.0	arrived at BRESLE + went into billets	/b
BRESLE	13/9 – 14/9		Received notice to vacate all billets + bivouac	
	15/9 – 16/9		Company fatigues, cleaning wagons etc., No. 4 section half day in camp in HENENCOURT wood	/b
	17/9 – 18/9		Standing by at 2 hours' notice. Erecting semi-permanent latrines in village	/b /b
	19/9	A.M. 7.0	Marched out of BRESLE.	/b
SHELTER WOOD		11.15	Arrived at SHELTER WOOD. A.D.S.+test press. Dugout bivouacs from 74th Field Coy. R.E.	/b

Army Form C. 2118.

(38)

WAR DIARY
or
INTELLIGENCE SUMMARY

102nd Field Company RE

1916

(Erase heading not required.)

Place	Date	Hour	Summary of Events and Information	Remarks and references to Appendices
SHELTER WOOD	19/9		I went up to MARTINPUICH to reconnoitre strong point near the MILL. Found a German attack on, and Brigade in consequence cancelled working parties.	p
	20/9		After discussion with CRE at 69th Brigade H.Q. Lieut. BIRD with one N.C.O. proceeded to headquarters of O.C. 11th West Yorkshire Regt. remained with the battalion for supervision of construction of new line forming strong points in advance of present front line on W. & N.W. of MARTINPUICH. Ireconnoitred strong point near The MILL, showing 2/Lieut. BURNELL what was required. No. 4 Section under the latter officer went up by night to wire, with a carrying party of 50 infantry. 70 yards of fairly strong entanglement completed. 8 men of No. 3 Section rebuilding an artillery O.P. by night.	p
	21/9		I went round site of new line in front of MARTINPUICH with O.C. 69th I.B. and CRE and subsequently marked out new strong point on E. side of MARTINPUICH MILL. No.s 1 & 4 Sections under Capt. ROBB and 2/Lieut. BURNELL went up by night to dig & wire it. The first dug turnphut to an average depth of 3'- & the apron of wire put out in front. No. 2 Section making conductors wire at THE CUTTING. 6 men of No. 3 Section repairing dug out near Brigade HQ. by day, and 8 on O.P. by night.	p

#353 Wt. W2544/f454 700,000 15/15 D. D | & L.   A.D.S.S./Forms/C. 2118.

WAR DIARY or INTELLIGENCE SUMMARY

Army Form C. 2118.

102nd Field Company R.E. (39)

1916

Place	Date	Hour	Summary of Events and Information	Remarks and references to Appendices
SHELTER WOOD	22/9		Nos 2 & 3 Sections - work as yesterday. Lieut. BIRD rejoined company on brigade relief. I went up in the morning stopped at new line ordered by C in C from MARTINPUICH HILL just to point on road N.E. of village (MARTINPUICH) on return found that orders to above were superseded by divisional order for barricade on the road referred to above and laying out of new line from E. end of sunken road at M 27 c 83 (Map GUEUDECOURT 57 c S.W. 1 1/10,000) to point where it is proposed to advance left flank of division on our right by to-nights attack - viz. M 27 D 64 (Approx). Capt. ROBB with No. 1 Section and 3 platoons of pioneers proceeded by night to carry out the work. They constructed barricade of wire & dug trench in connection therewith. Owing to brigade relief it was only possible to get 16 men from company in line at 1 a.m. who started strong point about 80x west of left flank of 50th Division line & threw out about 2' deep.	/o

Army Form C. 2118.

WAR DIARY *or* **INTELLIGENCE SUMMARY.**
(Erase heading not required.)

102nd Field Company R.E. (40)

1916

Place	Date	Hour	Summary of Events and Information	Remarks and references to Appendices
SHELTER WOOD	23/9		Nos 2 & 3 sections as yesterday. Artillery O.P. completed. I went up and taped out new line referred to in yesterday's diary to connect with new left flank of 50th Division. 2oo infantry (11th N.F.) digging line by night. Takes still line in advance of present line on N. edge of MARTINPUICH. [joining up] Strong points on the left to the MILL. 15o infantry (13th D.L.I.) digging line by night. No 1 & 4 sections with 3 platoons of pioneers as working party, under Capt. ROSS and Lieut BURWELL, improved barricade and strong point on EAUCOURT L'ABBÉ road in front of present front line. Progress good in line joining 50th Division, though to base of the latter was found. Line to west of mill was not touched owing to shelling and operations against 26th AVENUE.	
	24/9		No 2 section marking communication wires. No 3 section repairing dugouts. Inspected new trench on right flank, still finding no base of 50th Division.	©

Army Form C. 2118.

WAR DIARY or INTELLIGENCE SUMMARY

(Erase heading not required.)

102nd Field Company R.E.

1916

Place	Date	Hour	Summary of Events and Information	Remarks and references to Appendices
SHELTER WOOD	24/9 (contd)		Arranged to further work (deepening &c) in this trench by night. No work possible in trench to west of MINE owing to battalion relief. Nos 1 & 4 Sections (under 2/Lieut. BURWELL) with 3 platoons of pioneers, strengthened strong point at the MINE by night – working party of 20 pioneers dug new communication trench from this strong point in E. of MINE to join ZIG ZAG trench. Party of 100 infantry carried up wire and pickets. Excellent progress in spite of heavy shelling in early part of night. 2nd Lieut. BAXTER joined the company.	A
	25/9		No. 3 Section repairing dug outs. No. 4 in rest. Party turned out to make party laying out track studying trenches to pack mule halt to MARTINPUICH. Nos 1 & 2 Sections turned out for work by night under Capt. ROBB and 2/Lieut. CLARKE, but owing to the situation only 12 men of No. 1 Section were employed. The work ordered were as follows :—	B

WAR DIARY
INTELLIGENCE SUMMARY. 102nd Field Company R.E.

Army Form C. 2118.

(42)

1916

Place	Date	Hour	Summary of Events and Information	Remarks and references to Appendices
SHELTER WOOD	25/9 (contd)		3 Platoons of Pioneers to deepen so as to render tenable by daylight the trench running North West from M 26 B 53 (Map GUEUDECOURT 57C SW 1 1/10,000) and sappers to wire on West side of it, to an approx. distance of 150 yards. On arrival at site the point M 26 B 53 was found to be in German occupation as also a portion of the C.T. to that point. The Pioneers were therefore put on to deepen the switch trench from about M 26 B 61 towards M 26 B 73, while the sappers wired on N. side of this trench under heavy machine gun fire, completing 150+ of entanglement before receiving orders from the Brigade to retire about 12·30 A.M. They finally received orders to return home at 3 A.M. reaching camp at 6·0 A.M. No R.E. casualties, one Pioneer officer wounded.	
	26/9		No 1 Section resting after continuous spell of night work. No 3 Section repairing dug outs Nos 2 & 4 Sections under Capt ROSS and 2dLts BURWELL & CLARKE out laying	10

Army Form C. 2118.

WAR DIARY
or
INTELLIGENCE SUMMARY.

(43)

102nd Field Company RE

1916

(Erase heading not required.)

Place	Date	Hour	Summary of Events and Information	Remarks and references to Appendices
SHELTER WOOD	26/9 (contd)		night work 3 platoons of pioneers on following work:— No. 2 section and one platoon of pioneers improving barricade on EAUCOURT L'ABBÉ road. No. 4 section and one platoon of pioneers extending & strengthening wire round post on E. of MARTINPUICH MILL. One platoon of pioneers continuing communication trench from above post towards ZIGZAG trench in N.E. The line of an assembly trench running in an Easterly Direction from the ZIGZAG trench was taped out for a length of approx. 400'. Very little work possible after 1.0 P.M. owing to attack by division on our right. 2nd Lieut. O.R. slightly wounded. Capt. WHITFIELD being admitted to hospital, Sappers PEEK, SCOTT, and WATERS remaining at duty	fo
	27/9		No 1 section repairing dug outs No 4 " resting — erecting trench notice boards etc. No 2 Lieut. CLARKE proceeded to left Battalion HQR. to remain there in charge of normal daily working parties from battalions in the line.	

Army Form C. 2118.

WAR DIARY
or
INTELLIGENCE SUMMARY.
(Erase heading not required.)

1916. 102nd Field Company R.E.

Place	Date	Hour	Summary of Events and Information	Remarks and references to Appendices
SHELTER WOOD	27/9 (Contd)		Nos 2 & 3 sections under Lieut. BIRD and 2/Lieut. CLARKE, with 3 platoons of pioneers did the following work by night :— Constructed a strong point and block in trench taken this morning from the enemy on the right flank of our divisional front, viz: in 26th Avenue about M 27 A 89 (Sheet GUEUDECOURT 57 C SW1 1/10000).	
	28/9		No 1 section repairing & opening up dugouts in MARTINPUICH } by day. No 4 section making trench notice boards etc. No 3 section, with one platoon of pioneers, constructing new H.Q. for right battalion , by night. No 2 section with 2 platoons of pioneers preparing 2 advanced battalion H.Q. nearers assembly trench and superintending 2 companies of pioneers prevarating the lateral from the BAPAUME road to 26th Avenue in M 21 C & D (not as above)	

WAR DIARY or INTELLIGENCE SUMMARY

Army Form C. 2118.

102nd Field Company R.E.

(45)

1916

Place	Date	Hour	Summary of Events and Information	Remarks and references to Appendices
SHELTER WOOD	28/9 (cont.)		Casualties:- Sapper Anderson wounded. Owing to some misunderstanding, 2nd Lieut. CLARKE did not get the pioneers onto the site of work and to-day was done. Considerable shelling coincident with an abortive attack on DESTRÉMONT FARM.	
	29/9		After inspecting work, O.C. 70th Brigade in junction with the 50th Division on our right and DESTRÉMONT FARM, taken by us at 6 A.M. to-day, started digging a communication trench from 26th Avenue across to the FARM with one company 8th Yorks & Lancasters and two companies 9th Yorks & Lancasters. There were relieved about 3.0 P.M. by 2 companies of pioneers. By night, 2nd Lieuts. BURWELL & CLARKE with men from Nos 4 & 2 Sections respectively, 2 companies of pioneers, and 2 coy infantry from reserve brigade, went out to dig an outflank trench in East of DESTRÉMONT FARM across the front at the FARM. Owing to a bombing entrance on our right flank by the 50th Division	(2)

Army Form C. 2118.

WAR DIARY
or INTELLIGENCE SUMMARY.
(Erase heading not required.)

1916   102nd Field Company R.E.

(46)

Instructions regarding War Diaries and Intelligence Summaries are contained in F. S. Regs., Part II. and the Staff Manual respectively. Title pages will be prepared in manuscript.

Place	Date	Hour	Summary of Events and Information	Remarks and references to Appendices
SHELTER WOOD	29/9 (cont)		which besides being unsuccessful drew heavy retaliation from the enemy. The whole programme of work as arranged had to be altered, with the confusion inevitable to changing the disposition of large working parties in the dark under heavy shelling. Sind Wy Snie 270 yards were dug across the BAPAUME road. Cpl. McIntyre, Sapper Aldridge, Gibson & McCrea nil wounded. Cpl. Booth and Sapper Burgess wounded but remained at duty. 2nd. Cpl. Hill missing.	
	30/9		500 infantry cleaning out communication trenches by day. By night, 350 infantry and 200 pioneers under Capt. OUCHTERLONY and Lieut. BURWELL dug a second trench across from 26th Avenue to the North of BAPAUME road west of DESTREMONT FARM, about 50 yards in rear of trench dug yesterday, and joined the two trenches by a communication trench at a point 100 yards	fo

#353 Wt. W2544/1454 700,000 5/15 D. D. & L. A.D.S.S./Forms/C. 2118.

Army Form C. 2118.

WAR DIARY
or
INTELLIGENCE SUMMARY. 102nd Field Company R.E.

(47)

(Erase heading not required.)

Place	Date	Hour	Summary of Events and Information	Remarks and references to Appendices
SHELTER WOOD	30/9 (contd)		South of BAPAUME road. Nos. 1 & 3 Sections under Capt. ROSS and Lieut. BIRD moved to forward billets in HOOK TRENCH in readiness for the attack tomorrow on the LE SARS line. Capt. J.P.H. OUCHTERLONY wounded, but remains at duty. Sapper NAGGART wounded.	&

J.F. Mouchelony
Capt. R.E.
O.C. 102nd Field Company R.E.

WAR DIARY
INTELLIGENCE SUMMARY.

102nd Field Company R.E.

1916

(48)

Army Form C. 2118

Place	Date	Hour	Summary of Events and Information	Remarks and references to Appendices
SHELTER WOOD	1/10	P.M. 6.30	O.C. Company proceeded to 70th Brigade H.Q. to reconnoitre during the attack on LE SARS line which took place at 3.15 P.M. At 6.30 P.M. received orders from the division to send up sufficient Sappers to supervise construction of blocks in captured trenches on left flank. Capt. ROSS with 10 NCO's & sappers left Brigade H.Q.	
		6.55	at 6.55 P.M. & constructed blocks as follows:— In first captured line 250 x North of ALBERT–BAPAUME road. Second do do 30 x South do do do	10
	2/10	A.M. 3.45	Capt. ROSS reported at Brigade H.Q. on return. Lance Cpl. Ridgewell, Sappers Harris and Phillips wounded, but remain at duty	
		P.M. 9.0	3 companies of pioneers ordered up to dig communication trench from assaulting trench near DESTREMONT FARM to captured position. Received telegram from Capt. ROSS that the pioneers refused to above had been sent home by order of G.O.C. 69th Brigade	10

WAR DIARY
or
INTELLIGENCE SUMMARY. 102nd Field Company R.E.

1916

Army Form C. 2118.

Place	Date	Hour	Summary of Events and Information	Remarks and references to Appendices
SHELTER No D	3/10		Lines taped out to assembly trenches to North of DESTREMONT FARM and dug by night by pioneers.	
	4/10		Nos 1 & 3 Sections returned to headquarters from HOOK Trench Owing to postponement of operations due to the weather, no work done except the guiding of an infantry party carrying R.E. Stores	
	5/10		Nos 2 & 4 Sections under 2/Lieut. BAXTER assisting O.C. 128th Field Coy R.E. on laying of tramline. Lieut. BIRD supervising pioneer work in 69th Bde Area. 2/Lieut CLARKE at disposal of 68th Bde. to give assistance in laying out new line.	
	6/10		Standing by for orders. 2/Lieut CLARKE with 6 sappers reported to 68th Bde at 7.0 P.M. to work tonight in the front of their attack on THE TANGLE being successful. It was not.	
	7/10		Divisional attack on and capture of LE SARS. Nos 3 & 4 sections at disposal of 69th Brigade. No 1 section at disposal of 68th Brigade.	

Army Form C. 2118.

WAR DIARY
or
INTELLIGENCE SUMMARY. 102nd Field Company R.E.
(Erase heading not required.)

(50)

1916

Instructions regarding War Diaries and Intelligence Summaries are contained in F. S. Regs., Part II. and the Staff Manual respectively. Title pages will be prepared in manuscript.

Place	Date	Hour	Summary of Events and Information	Remarks and references to Appendices
SHELTER WOOD	7/10 (cont.)		Nos 3 & 4 sections constructed strong points on North side of HESSIAN, No. 1 section employed in general consolidation work.	/o
	8/10		Sergt. Redolph wounded. Company resting and packing up ready for relief. Sergt. Redolph awarded the Military Medal	/o
	9/10	A.M. 9.45	Handed over work to 73rd Field Coy. and billets to 91st Field Coy.	/o
ALBERT	10/10		Marched out from SHELTER WOOD to ALBERT Resting in billets. Lieut. BIRD and 10 O.R. proceeded to new area as advanced billeting party.	/o
	11/10	P.M. 4.45	Left ALBERT by train. Sergt. HUDSON & Cpl. HENSON awarded Military Medals.	/o
	12/10	A.M. 7.0	Detrained at LONG-PRÉ & marched to billets at FAMECHON, arriving 9.15 a.m.	
FAMECHON		P.M. 7.45	Transport proceeding by road from ALBERT, halted for night of 11/12 at ARGOEUVES and arrived at FAMECHON at 4.15 p.m.	/o
		Noon 12.0	Received orders from 69th Brigade to march tomorrow to ST RIQUIER	
	13/10	P.M. 2.0	Marched out of FAMECHON	/o
ST. RIQUIER	14/10		Arrived at ST. RIQUIER & went into billets Company fatigues	/o/

Army Form C. 2118.

(51)

WAR DIARY
or
INTELLIGENCE SUMMARY.
(Erase heading not required.)

102nd Field Company R.E.

1916

Place	Date	Hour	Summary of Events and Information	Remarks and references to Appendices
ST. RIQUIER	15/10	P.M. 12.15	Marched out to CONTEVILLE Station. Left by rail at 6.0 p.m. arriving	
	16/10		HOUPOUTRE 12.15 AM 16/10. Detrained & marched to billets in RENINGHELST - VLAMERTINGHE road. Took over work from 5th Australian Field Company	b/f
R.E. Camp on RENINGHELST - VLAMERTINGHE road.	17/10 18/10 - 31/10 19/10 22/10		Took over camp from 5th Australian Field Company, & continued taking over work. Company distributed in numerous works - hutting, horse standings, renewing tramways etc. 2/Lieut. A.M. CLARKE admitted to hospital - heart trouble. Corpml Book, 2nd Corpml McIntyre, Lance Cpls. Hooper and Chambers, Sappers Medose, Polkinghorne and Seagrove awarded Military Medals	b/f b/f b/f b/f

J.P.O'Connell(?)
Capt R.E.
O.C. 102nd Field Company R.E.

Secret

Vol 14

War Diary   November
102nd Fd Coy R.E.

Army Form C. 2118.

WAR DIARY
or
INTELLIGENCE SUMMARY.
(Erase heading not required.)

102nd Field Company RE

(52)

1916

Place	Date	Hour	Summary of Events and Information	Remarks and references to Appendices
R.E. Camp on road OUDERDOM -VLAMERTINGHE	1/11 -30/11		Company employed in the back area erecting huts, stables etc for winter accommodation, working in the shops in R.E. Brit. Dump, relaying tramline past ZILLEBECKE pond etc.	
	15/11		2 Lieut. S.M. SAUNDERS joined company from base.	
	29/11		2 Lieut. S.R. TYSSEN rejoined company from base	

J.P. Houldsworth
Capt R.E.
OC 102nd Field Company R.E.

Vol 15

Secret

War Diary
of
102nd Field Coy R.E
for month of
DECEMBER.

Army Form C. 2118.

(53)

WAR DIARY
INTELLIGENCE SUMMARY. 102nd Field Company R.E.
(Erase heading not required.)

1916

Place	Date	Hour	Summary of Events and Information	Remarks and references to Appendices
R.E. camp on road OUDERDOM + LAMERTINGHE	1/12 – 31/12		No. 2 Section under Lieut. SAUNDERS on repairs and improvements to tram line from BRISBANE DUMP to HELL BLAST CORNER. Nos 1, 3, & 4 sections on hutting, stabling etc. in reserve area, divisional workshops etc.	
	7/12		Capt. OUCHTERLONY took over duties of Acting C.R.E.	
	21/12		Major OUCHTERLONY resumed command of company	
	31/12		Lieut. BIRD left company on appointment to the WORKS DIRECTORATE	

J.W. Ouchterlony
Major R.E.
O.C. 102nd Field Coy R.E.

Confidential

Vol 16

War Diary
of
102nd Fd Coy R.E
from January 1st 1917 to January 31st 1917

Army Form C. 2118.

WAR DIARY
or
INTELLIGENCE SUMMARY.
(Erase heading not required.)

102nd Field Company RE (54)

1917

Place	Date	Hour	Summary of Events and Information	Remarks and references to Appendices
R.E. Camp, OUDERDOM	1/1 – 3/1	–	No. 3 Section (2/Lieut. TYSSEN) underpinning and strengthening cellars in KRUISSTRAAT.	
VLAMERTINGHE road	1/1 – 3/1	–	No. 2 Section (2/Lieut. SAUNDERS) relaying tram line near ZILLEBEKE.	
	4/1	–	No. 2 Section – Small detachment making new siding and ammunition dump near VLAMERTINGHE – remainder of section working with No. 3 Section (as above).	
	1/1		Remainder of company erecting various huts etc. in back area, running saws and shops in divisional dump etc.	
	2/1		Major OUCHTERLONY joined R.E. School of Instruction, GHQ for short course.	
	10/1		" rejoined company on completion of course.	
	22/1		2/Lieut BAXTER proceeded on leave to England.	
	26/1		Capt. ROBB " " "	
	28/1		Major OUCHTERLONY joined RE School of Instruction GHQ as instructor.	
			2/Lt. H.P. NYE (T.C.) joined company for duty.	

Powell Burnell
Lieut. RE
a/O.C. 102nd Field Coy. RE.

Vol 17

CONFIDENTIAL

War Diary
of
102nd Field Coy R.E.

from 1st February 1917 — 28 February 1917

VOLUMES 55 & 56

Army Form C. 2118.

WAR DIARY
or
INTELLIGENCE SUMMARY.
(Erase heading not required)

102nd Field Co. R.E.

1917

Place	Date	Hour	Summary of Events and Information	Remarks and references to Appendices
R.E Camp OUDERDOM	1/2		No. 2 Section (2/Lieut SAUNDERS) making ammunition dump near VLAMERTINGHE	
-VLAMERTINGHE road.	1/2		No. 3 Section (2/Lieut TYSSEN) strengthening cellars at KRUISSTRAAT.	
	1/2		Sections 1 & 4 erecting huts in hut area	DnR.
	3/2		Capt D. G. ROBB returned from leave to England and assumed Command of the Co.	DnR
	6/2		MAJOR E H ROOKE took over CRE's duties. COL A G BREINER opposite CE XIX Corps.	
	6/2		Nos 2 & 3 Sections making Div. Amm. Refilling Pt near VLAMERTINGHE. Nos 1 & 4 erecting huts, various RE works. 2Lt BAXTER returning from leave.	DnR
	8/2		2Lt NYE attached to 128th Fld Co RE. for duty	DnR
	14/2		2Lt SAUNDERS attached to CRE (in duty as) Asst acting adjutant	DnR
	19/2		2Lt. TYSSEN admitted Div. Rest Station, near	
	20/2		C.S.M. BURRIDGE presented with Meritorious Service Medal by Corps Commander (Gen MORLAND). (London Gazette 2 Jan. 17).	DnR
	23/2		Advance Party of Relieving Coy (234 II Fld Co RE.) arrived in Camp. Works handed over to CAPT. MARSTON RE OC 234 II Fld Co RE.	DnR
			2Lt NYE returns to duty from 128th Fld Co RE.	

Army Form C. 2118.

WAR DIARY
or
INTELLIGENCE SUMMARY.
(Erase heading not required.)

(56)

102nd Field Co R.E.

1917

Place	Date FEBRUARY	Hour	Summary of Events and Information	Remarks and references to Appendices
REC Camp OUDERDOM	24	12 noon	Hand over camp etc to relieving unit 234th Fld Co RE, 35th Division	DHR.
VLAMERTINGHE Road		7 am	Transport (Lt. BURWELL) march out en route to billets at LEDERZEELE	DHR.
		12.30 p.m.	Coy march out of camp, entrain at POPERINGHE, detrain at BOLLEZEELE, & march into billets at LEDERZEELE. (move with 70th Bgde)	DHR.
LEDERZEELE	25	10.30	Whole Coy. march to BAYENGHEM-LES-EPERLECQUES	DHR.
BAYENGHEM	26	10.30	Whole Coy. route march to TOURNEHEM.	DHR.
TOURNEHEM	27		Settling down in billets (2 hrs squad drill etc in morning)	DHR.
"	28		Squad Drill, & Company Drill, morning & afternoon	

D.H. Roth. Capt R.E.
O.C. 102 Fld Co R.E.

WAR DIARY
or
INTELLIGENCE SUMMARY.

Army Form C. 2118.

Vol / 8

(57)

102nd Field Co R.E.

1917

Place	Date MARCH	Hour	Summary of Events and Information	Remarks and references to Appendices
TOURNEHEM	1–17.		Survey training, incoding Bridges, wiring, Demolition & Sections Schemes.	D.W.R.
	3		2 Lt S.R.D.Tyser rejoined Coy. from Hospital. Capt Robb a. O.C. matures.	D.W.R.
	12		2 Lt S.R.D.Tyser admitted C.C.S., sick.	D.W.R
	15		Completed construction of Bath Houses in Belgium	D.W.R
	18		Recce orders for move to BOLEZEELE area (70th Bgde O.O.)	D.W.R
	19		Coy. Parade 8.50 a.m. for march south to BAYENGHEM-LES-EPERLECQUES	D.W.R
BAYENGHEM LES EPERLECQUES	20		Coy. Parade 8 a.m. for march North to BROXEELE	D.W.R
BROXEELE	21		Coy. Parade 8.15 a.m. for march North to HERZEELE area arrives in Billets in BAMBECQUE (3.30 pm)	D.W.R
BAMBECQUE	22		Camp Fatigues	D.W.R
	23		Section Training	
	24		E.Brunell & 245 Boots & 40 O.R. (mostly Sects I & IV) leave BAMBECQUE to report to CE VIII Corps for work in Int & line. 70th Bgde Officers & NCO's in matures in Defences of Villages	D.W.R.
			Capt Robb a. O.C. matures 70th Bgde Officers & NCO's in Defence of Villages	D.W.R

Army Form C. 2118.

WAR DIARY
or
INTELLIGENCE SUMMARY.

(Erase heading not required.)

Instructions regarding War Diaries and Intelligence Summaries are contained in F. S. Regs., Part II. and the Staff Manual respectively. Title pages will be prepared in manuscript.

102ⁿᵈ Field Co. R.E.   58

1917

Place	Date MARCH	Hour	Summary of Events and Information	Remarks and references to Appendices
BAMBECQUE	24		Major T.P.H. Chesterton resumes Command of Company from R.E. School of Instruction	D.R.
	26		Major T.P.H. Chesterton is in attendance a executing to the On. Rest Station on the 30ᵗʰ.	D.R.
	24 & 30		Shoeing Training	D.R.
	31		Coy. marches out of billets in BAMBECQUE 9.30 a.m. to billets in LEDRINGHEM.	D.R.
LEDRINGHEM				

D.H. Roth. Capt. R.E.
a/o.c. 102ⁿᵈ Fld Co. R.E.

WAR DIARY
or
INTELLIGENCE SUMMARY

Army Form C. 2118.

Vol 79

102nd FIELD CO. R.E.

APRIL 1917

Place	Date	Hour	Summary of Events and Information	Remarks and references to Appendices
LEDRENGHEM	1-3		General Training. 2/Lt R.H. TAYLOR. R.E (T.C) joins the Coy from the area.	DnR
	4		March out of LEDRENGHEM (Co board) to WILL'S S. of WATOU MAJOR OUGHTERLONY coming from hospital & assumes command of Co.	DnR
WATOU AREA			One 2 officers & 40 O.R. Company relieved C.E. VIII Corps signal Coy.	DnR
	6	P.M. 2.0	March out of Wheb - WATOU area - proceed to hutts W. of RENINGHELST.	Jo.Co.
RENINGHELST AREA	7		Arranging taking over from 518th Field Company R.E. 47th Division	
BELGIAN CHATEAU	8		Completed taking over HILL 60 Sector from 518th Field Company R.E. + work on Machine gun emplacements from 517th Field Company R.E.	
		P.M. 2.0	Company marched out of camp near RENINGHELST.	
		8.30	Company arrived in new huts - dugouts near Belgian Chateau	Jo
	9		No 2 Section started work on extension of RAILWAY dugouts. Remainder of Company repairing huts etc. and reconnoitring new work	Jo

Army Form C. 2118.

WAR DIARY
or
INTELLIGENCE SUMMARY.
(Erase heading not required.)

1917 60 / 102nd Field Company RE

Place	Date	Hour	Summary of Events and Information	Remarks and references to Appendices
BELGIAN CHATEAU	10/4 – 16/4			
	10/4		No. 3 Section on extension of RAILWAY Dugouts. Nos 1, 2, 4 sections assisting Right Battalion (8th Yorks & Lancs), No 2 section the Centre Battalion (11th Notts & Derby) to relevein damaged trenches in front line system.	
	11/4		2nd Lieut. Hidey and Lieut. Withington with 50 O.R. of 8th Yorkshire Regiment & 2nd Lieuts. KING and ROBERTS with 50 O.R. of 11th West Yorks Regiment joined the company on temporary attachment for work. Work as for 10/4.	p.
	12/4		Work as for 10/4 with the addition of supervision of pioneers on wiring the support line, starting from the right flank.	p.
	13/4		No. 2 Section moved up to billets in ZILLEBEKE BUND under point NYE. Work as for 10/4 inst. Front line of centre battalion made passable throughout. 2 foot cubes destroyed by shell fire.	p.
	14/4		Work as for 10/4; somewhat impeded by relief of 70th Bde. by 69th Bde. Sapper Buckley + one attached infantryman killed, and six attached infantrymen wounded by antiaircraft shell near RAILWAY DUGOUTS. 2nd Lieut. WITHINGTON 8th Yorks Battalion wounded by T.M. fire.	p.

Army Form C. 2118.

WAR DIARY
or
INTELLIGENCE SUMMARY.
(Erase heading not required.)

102nd Field Company R.E.

1917

(61)

Place	Date	Hour	Summary of Events and Information	Remarks and references to Appendices
BELGIAN CHATEAU	15/4		No. 1 Section (2/Lt BAXTER) took over work in OBSERVATORY RIDGE sector from 128th Field Company R.E. Remainder of work as for 10/4.	do
YPRES	16/4		Company moved to new billets in YPRES, the attached infantry being billeted in KRUISSTRAAT.	do
	17/4–19/4		Distribution of company to work was as follows: Nos 1, 2, & 1 Section working respectively in Right, Centre, & Left Battalion sectors, repairing damaged trenches, drainage etc. No. 3 section on extension of Railway Dugouts and construction of Signal station dug out in ZILLEBEKE BUND.	do
	20/4		Handed over work in OBSERVATORY RIDGE (MOUNT SORREL) Sector to O.C. 128th Field Company R.E.. No. 1 Section (2/Lieut. BAXTER) returned to work on Right of Divisional Front (South of Hill 60 to WINDY CORNER). Remainder the section of 128th Field Company R.E. under Lieut COPE attached to the company for work — employed on relaxation of WANGARATTA Trench and drainage & repairs to VERBET RIDGE, METROPOLITAN NEFT and ZILLEBEKE Switch. "B" Coy. 9th South Staffords ("Pioneers") attached for work in company sector 20/4	do
	21/4		Distribution of company as for 20/4	do

WAR DIARY
or
INTELLIGENCE SUMMARY
(Erase heading not required.)

Army Form C. 2118.

62 102nd Field Company R.E.

1917

Place	Date	Hour	Summary of Events and Information	Remarks and references to Appendices
YPRES	22/4 - 26/4		Detail of work as for 20/4.	/c /c
	25/4		Sappers BOLTON and WHEELER wounded.	
	27/4		Corp. Burridge struck off strength of company on being invalided. No 2 section 128th Field Company R.E. (under Lieut. COPE) and left of 'B' Coy. 9th South Staffs (Pioneers) transferred to work in Left Brigade Sector (HOOGE) under O.C. 128th Field Company R.E.	/c
	28/4		2/Lieut. B.P. GAYMER joined company from base.	/c
	29/4		2/Lieuts. H.P. NYE and B.P. GAYMER wounded but remain at duty. Received orders to prepare to hand over to relieving Field Coy. at short notice.	/c /c
	30/4		No 1 section marched from YPRES to transport lines to load wagons etc. Clearing up and preparing to hand over to 82nd Field Coy., 19th Div's.	/c /c

JP Mitchwhulm Major R.E.
O.C. 102nd Field Coy R.E.

WAR DIARY
INTELLIGENCE SUMMARY
(Erase heading not required.)

102nd Field Company R.E.

Vol 20

1917

Place	Date	Hour	Summary of Events and Information	Remarks and references to Appendices
YPRES	1/5		Handed over work and billets to 82nd Field Company, 19th Division.	
WINNIPEG CAMP	2/5	A.M. 10.0	Company marched to WINNIPEG camp, near OUDERDOM	fo
		P.M. 1.0	Company marched out from WINNIPEG camp. Company arrived in billets near BOESCHEPE	fo
BOESCHEPE	3/5		Company inspected by Major General Sir J.M. Babington K.C.M.G. C.B. G.O.C. 23rd Div:-	fo
	4/5		Overhauling & cleaning company equipment.	fo
	5/5		General training. Attached infantry of 19th Brigade returned to their units. One platoon from each battalion of 70th Brigade joined the company for one months attachment.	fo
	6/5 - 9/5		General training - defence of woods and villages, R.E. Reconnaissance, pontoon drill, rapid wiring etc.	fo
	9/5		Received orders to proceed to YPRES on 10th inst. & take over from 82nd Field Coy. R.E. 19th Div:n in still bo sector.	fo
YPRES	10/5		Company marched from BOESCHEPE to YPRES and took over work, billets etc. from 82nd Field Company R.E.	fo
		P.M. 10.45	Relief completed.	fo

Army Form C. 2118.

WAR DIARY
INTELLIGENCE SUMMARY.
(Erase heading not required.)

102nd Field Company R.E.

64

1917

Place	Date	Hour	Summary of Events and Information	Remarks and references to Appendices
YPRES	11/5		Reconnoitring work, which started on night 11/12.	
			Distribution — No 1 & 4 Section in Right Battalion sector) preparing for	
			No. 2 " Centre ") Offensive	
			No. 3 " "	
			Dugout in extension of Railway dugouts, signal	fo
	12/5		dugout in ZILLEBEKE Bund, and rear work generally	fo
			Brigade in the sector (Hill 60) — 68th Brigade	fo
			Sapper FORDHAM H. wounded — & died in Field Ambulance	fo
	13/5		No 2 Section, 128th Field Company under Lieut COPE, inc. attached infantry	fo
			attached for work.	fo
	15/5		Sapper McINTYRE wounded.	fo
	16/5		Corporal PIERCE appointed Acting Foreman of Works	fo
	17/5		In addition to work as for 11/5 & succeeding days, dug new trench in	
			front of Hill 60 between two front line posts after successful explosion	
			of mine. Length 75 x. Party — 45 men into 2 officers, 13th D.L.I. Party	
			On work at 1.15 am & withdrew out 3.30 a.m.	fo
	18/5		Capt. ROBB proceeded on special leave. 2nd Lt. GAYTHER taking over	fo
			his duties	

Army Form C. 2118.

WAR DIARY
or
INTELLIGENCE SUMMARY.
(Erase heading not required.)

102nd Field Company R.E. (65)

1917

Place	Date	Hour	Summary of Events and Information	Remarks and references to Appendices
YPRES	MAY 18/19		69th Brigade relieved 68th Brigade in Hill 60 sector	do
	19		Major OUCHTERLONY, Captain ROBB, and LIEUT. BURNELL mentioned in C in C's despatch dated April 9th.	do
	21		2nd Lieut R.H. TAYLOR and Sapper BARLOW wounded	do
	24/25		70th Brigade relieved 69th Brigade in Hill 60 sector	do
	25		Sapper CLARKE W. killed by shell in WANGARATTA Trench	do
	24		Lieut. R.G. CHRISTIE temporarily attached to supervise transport lines and supply of stores. 2nd Lieut GAYMER assumed command of No. 3 Section	do do
	27		Sapper BARRATT, H. wounded	do
	28		Sapper CUMMINGS, W.A. wounded	do
			Lance Cpl. LOWE, Sapper BIGNELL, A., ELLIOT, W., FLETCHER, T., and JACKSON, F. wounded	do
			Captain ROBB returned from leave	do
	29		Sapper ELLIOT died of wounds in C.C.S.	do
	31		Preparations for offensive practically complete. From this date only maintenance	

Army Form C. 2118.

WAR DIARY
INTELLIGENCE SUMMARY
(Erase heading not required.)

(66) 102nd Field Company RE

Place	Date	Hour	Summary of Events and Information	Remarks and references to Appendices
YPRES	MAY 31		maintenance required.	
			Lieut. COPE and N° 2 Section 128th Field Company ceased to be attached to the company for work.	
	May/June 31/1		2/Lieut. W.G. LANG-ANDERSON joined the company in first appointment.	A
			68th Brigade relieved 70th Brigade in Hill 60 Sector	A

JPWockelond
Major RE
O.C. 102nd Field Coy RE

WAR DIARY or INTELLIGENCE SUMMARY.
(Erase heading not required.)

Army Form C. 2118.

(67)

102nd Field Company R.E.

Vol 21

1917

Place	Date	Hour	Summary of Events and Information	Remarks and references to Appendices
YPRES	JUNE 1		Company employed on maintenance of assembly & communication trenches, forward dumps, water points etc.	
	2		Driver Yates wounded and died two hours later	
	3		Lieut. BURNELL wounded	
	4		Major OUCHTERLONY awarded the D.S.O. in Kings Birthday Honours	
	5	P.M. 11.0	O.C. 69th Brigade assumed command of Hill 60 sector	
	6		Nos 1, 2 & 4 Sections assemble in the PROMENADE TRENCH in ZILLEBEKE. Sapper Bell wounded	D.W.R.
	7		LAKE 2.30 p.m. (2 Lieuts Baxter, Nye & Anderson) 2nd Army attack 3.10 a.m. MAJOR OUCHTERLONY D.S.O. killed in the afternoon near Allen Gates. Sections 1, 2 & 4 leave assembly Trenches for work 5.30 p.m. CAPTAIN ROBB assumes command of Co. Section 1 (2Lt. BAXTER) construct a strong point, junction IMPACT SUPPORT & IMPACT AVENUE (50 12th D.L.I. carrying) Sect 2. (2Lt. NYE) constructs a post at IMMOVABLE SUPPORT C.I. Redoubt Pioneers, 2 Platoons all Infantry carrying) Sect 4 (2Lt ANDERSON) constructs a strong point, S.E. End of CATERPILLAR	D.W.R.

WAR DIARY
or
INTELLIGENCE SUMMARY.
(Erase heading not required.)

Army Form C. 2118.

68

102nd Field Co R.E.

Instructions regarding War Diaries and Intelligence Summaries are contained in F. S. Regs., Part II. and the Staff Manual respectively. Title pages will be prepared in manuscript.

Place	Date	Hour	Summary of Events and Information	Remarks and references to Appendices
HILL 60	JUNE 7-8		(1 Platoon Pioneers + 2 Platoons oth Infantry assisting)	
			4 Platoons Pioneers dugging Communication Trenches, 1 from SWIFT STREET	DuR
			+ 1 from ALLEN CRATER To IMMOVABLE TRENCH.	
			R.E. Section returns To rests in YPRES at 4 a.m.	
	8-9		1 Section (No 3. 2Lt GAYMER) proceed To construct S.P. in junction of	DuR
			IMMOVABLE SUPPORT & IMMEDIATE AVENUE as owing to hostile barrage work was	
			impossible. Part of IMMOVABLE SUPPORT was unnecessarily weak.	
			2 went P.S. Hudson (Territorials force) joined the Co. from the base for duty	
	9-10		2 Sections (No 2 2Lt NYE + No 4 2Lt ANDERSON) were on strong point and	DuR
			support line relined IMPARTIAL TRENCH (I 36 a) 60 (approx.) Infantry assisting.	
			6 Platoons Pioneers were on support line.	
	10-11		2 Sections (No 4 2Lt ANDERSON + No 3 2Lt GAYMER) at work on No 4 wing	
			Strong Point in the Support Line. No 3 M.G. function on Ry Cutting opposite	DuR
			support line were continually delayed with by shell fire	
	11-12		2Lt NYE + 7 sappers from Section 2 were out there in front of BATTLE WOOD	
			To join up unconnected parts of front line. The infantry working party	

WAR DIARY
or
INTELLIGENCE SUMMARY.
(Erase heading not required.)

Army Form C. 2118.

102nd Field Co. R.E.

Place	Date	Hour	Summary of Events and Information	Remarks and references to Appendices
YPRES	JUNE			
			Field to complete. No.101395 Sapper LACE R. wounded. No.103098 Sapper GILES P.C. (wounded returned at duty)	DuR
	12	8 pm	#4 Coy marched out of billets in YPRES to Coy Transport lines, BRANDHOEK	DuR
			ROAD. 69th Bgde. 23 Div. relieved by 17th Bgde. 24 Div.	
	13	11 am	Whole Coy marches from TRANSPORT LINES to camp near DICKEBUSCH. (motor lorries)	DuR
			O.C. Coy reports at 17th Bgde. Cdo. H.Q. (B.G. STONE) for instructions as	
	14 14/15 DuR		R.E. work for attack on following night. These instructions were deferred to	DuR
			CRE were consequently modified	
	14/15		O.C. Coy at Bgde H.Q. (Cdo.) 17th Bgde. 2 complete sections (2nd LT NYE & 2nd LT HUDSON) work in forward area near JACKSONS DUMP on forward accommodation for Coy. 2nd LT ANDERSON, 2nd LT GAYMER, & 12 Sappers instructed to consolidate Railway points in front line if newly gained objective. They proceed to work with 50 Infantry attached to each officer at 10 pm – 2nd LT ANDERSON to construct a wire two strong points in front of BATTLE WOOD in account of hostile barrage	DuR

WAR DIARY
or
INTELLIGENCE SUMMARY.
(Erase heading not required.)

Army Form C. 2118.

102nd Field Co. RE.

Place	Date	Hour	Summary of Events and Information	Remarks and references to Appendices
DICKEBUSCH	JUNE			
			2Lt ANDERSON rang O.C Coy up & asked for instructions. O.C 17th Bny. conveying O.C Coy orders 2Lt ANDERSON to return to Bny HQ with the party, any work being excavated impossible.	
			2Lt ANDERSON returned to Bny HQ at 3 a.m.	
			2Lt GAYMER and his party proceed to the site for the story 200ft feet in front of IMPARTIAL TRENCH & succeeded in consolidating the story posts. 2Lt GAYMER reported at Bny HQ. at 4.a.m. No 145535 Sapper ELLIS H. (wounded remains at duty)	D/R
	15 5pm to 5am		2Lt NYE & 2Lt HUDSON return to camp at DICKEBUSCH at 11 a.m. Coy. Hand over work to O.C. 104th Field Co RE (24 Div.)	D/R
	16 6am		Coy. marches out of camp at DICKEBUSCH to town near BERTHEN	
BERTHEN area.	17		Coy. march	
	18		Coy. inspected and congratulated on work done by G.O.C. 23 Division. The following N.C.O's & men awarded decorations (X corps R.O.(No.1115) D.R.O. 2757 dated 16/6/17) No 56527 Cpl (a/Sergt) T. BOOTH 102 Fd MM	D/R

WAR DIARY
or
INTELLIGENCE SUMMARY.

(Erase heading not required.)

Army Form C. 2118.

(71)

102nd Field Co. R.E.

Place	Date	Hour	Summary of Events and Information	Remarks and references to Appendices
	JUNE			
BERTHEN area	18		No 56233 L/Cpl J. MELROSE been to H.M., Military Medal to 51280 Spr BRYARS, 53047 L/Cpl LAWSON, 53044 Spr McDOWELL, 100321 Spr AUSTIN, 56531 Spr HARRIS, 56512 Spr WELLINGS, 51640 Spr PHILLIPS, 150032 Spr BINSTEAD, 51886 Spr BAINBRIDGE, 51286 Spr BREWIS	DnR.
			CAPT D.C.ROBB, O.C Coy. given authority to wear MAJOR'S RANK	DnR
BERTHEN area	19		Kit inspection & checking stores.	
	20		General inspection of tools & equipment	DnR
			CAPT J. KIDDELL R.E. reported for duty as second-in-command of the Coy.	
			2 Lieut H.P. NYE proceeds on leave to ENGLAND	
	21		General camp fatigues etc	
	22		evacuation to No7 General Hospital (Reims) 2 Lieut P.S. HUDSON R.E. (T.P.)	
	23		2 Lieut H.P. NYE R.E. awarded the Military Cross	DnR
			Coy Sports	
	24			
	25		General camp fatigues. 2 Lieut E.E BAXTER proceeds on leave to U.K.	DnR
	26		Camp fatigues in morning. Range practice (200x) in afternoon	DnR

WAR DIARY
or
INTELLIGENCE SUMMARY.
(Erase heading not required.)

Army Form C. 2118.

102nd Field Co. R.E. (72)

Place	Date	Hour	Summary of Events and Information	Remarks and references to Appendices
	JUNE			
BERTHEN	27		Rifle firing on Rifle Range. The whole Co. put through.	
AREA	28		Packing up & loading wagons etc. Capt RIGGELL & Lieut GAYMER	DNR
	28		left on leave	
	29	6am	Coy marched out of BERTHEN AREA to the BURGOMASTER'S FARM. G.O.C. Div. wants to address officers & warrant officers & N.C.Os from 104th Field Co (24th Div) &	
DICKEBUSCH				
near DICKEBUSCH.			Took over work on the line from 104th Field Co R.E.	DNR
			3 Sections (2 Lieuts LANG-ANDERSON & GAYMER) proceed to the	
			to Lectte in SPOIL BANK (Tunnels) working with 69th Brigade.	
	30		See G.O.C. 69th Brigade re work in the line. Also work in	DNR
SPOIL BANK				
			C.T. OAK LANE system. Proceed on C.T. IMPACT AVENUE System	

D.M. Rob
Major R.E.
O.C. 102 Field Co R.E.

Army Form C. 2118.

WAR DIARY
or
INTELLIGENCE SUMMARY.
(Erase heading not required.)

(13) 102nd Field Co R.E. Vol 22

Instructions regarding War Diaries and Intelligence Summaries are contained in F. S. Regs., Part II. and the Staff Manual respectively. Title pages will be prepared in manuscript.

Place	Date	Hour	Summary of Events and Information	Remarks and references to Appendices
	JULY			
DICKEBUSCH	1		1 Section working on tactical wire DICKEBUSCH Nos 2, 3, 4 Sections work on C.T. OAK LANE Saptins, 2 C.T. IMPERIAL AVENUE Saptins. Sites for R.A.P's, B.H.Q. H.Q. reconnoitred. Preparations front for 41st Division.	DMR.
SPOIL BANK	2		2 hours H.P. N.Y.E. M.C. returns from leave. Work as on 1st. No 62046 Sapper GREGORY I wounded in duty.	
	3		Received orders to hand over sector (SPOIL BANK & BATTLE WOOD) to 512th Fd Co 47 Div. To proceed to forward billets in LARCH WOOD Tunnels to work in 2 ft section of the two divisional front. To accommodation ready to LARCH WOOD TUNNELS, 2nd Coy return to BURGOMASTER'S FARM for night. 3/4. 2 hour long draw on – 20 Sapper work in tunnels to prepare billets for the Coy. No 51645 Sapper COWAN R. wounded.	DMR.
	4		Coy ens No 1 Section proceed to forward billets in LARCH WOOD Tunnels. Work commenced on Assembly Trenches, Communication Trenches, 2 R.A.P.'s. Preparations for the 24th Division offensive. Work in conjunction with 70th Bgde. Sect 1 & 2 hard work – Andrews's reconnoitre Sect. 3 (2 hours NYE MG) in the work in the eye hole of the Coy. Section Sect. 2 (2 hours NYE MG) – Shewin agitation important, Sect. 3 (2 hours Grayman) work on R.A.P.'s.	DMR.

Army Form C. 2118.

WAR DIARY
or
INTELLIGENCE SUMMARY.
(Erase heading not required.)

102nd Field Co. R.E.   (74)

Instructions regarding War Diaries and Intelligence Summaries are contained in F. S. Regs., Part II. and the Staff Manual respectively. Title pages will be prepared in manuscript.

Place	Date	Hour	Summary of Events and Information	Remarks and references to Appendices
	JULY			
LARCH WOOD	5		100 XXX reports from 69th Bgde attd to Coy for work on the 2 Midgey	
TUNNELS			work on respective communications, men returned with it at dusk fire	SMR
			No 32591 D. WEIR G. wounded at duty	
	6		D Coy 5th S Staffs (Capt LISTER) have now instructions from O.E. Coy	
			work on C.T.s, Support & Reserve Lines & Aramenty Tunnel.	
			No. 56531 Sapper HARRIS S. wounded, No 82053 Sapper HOLLOWAY W.	SMR
			died of wounds, No 18260 Sapper HIND T. killed	
			work on completion with 68th Bgde. 2 hrs E.E. BAXTER relieve him leave	
	7		hours as usual. No. 56510 2nd Lipl HUSH W. wounded at duty	
	8		work as usual, repairing & cleaning of obstructions, frontline support	SMR
	9		and Aramenty Trenches, communication trenches & CTs.	
	10		as above. 2 hrs HP NYE M.C. wounded at duty	
			2 Corpl D. Y. L. (Capt Cocke D.S.O.) hrt Claurins M.C.) attd	
			to Coy for work on LARCH WOOD Aramenty Tunnels.	SMR
	11		Sect 1 (2 Lieut BAXTER) relieve Sect 2 (2 Lieut NYE MC) on	
			forward trench work over the work of Sect 2.	

Army Form C. 2118.

WAR DIARY
or
INTELLIGENCE SUMMARY.
(Erase heading not required.)

102nd Field Coy RE (75)

Place	Date	Hour	Summary of Events and Information	Remarks and references to Appendices
	JULY			
LARCH WOOD				
TUNNELS	12		Work as usual but much interfered with by shell fire	OHR
	13		do. 2 Cpls of Y.& L rejoin their unit on completion of task	
	14		2 Lieut GAYNER injured at duty. Relieving by 2nd Lieut 20th NF	
	15		do. No 51072 Cpl HOOPER R. wounded at duty	
	16		do.	OHR
	17		do. No 51539 Spr WYNNE T. wounded at duty. No 48748 Mtr Cpl DUDLEY C.	
	18		2 Lieut KANE-ANDERSON wounded	
	19		Work as usual	
	20		do. Lieut FAIRBAIRN RE (103rd Field Co RE) & 10 sappers report at Coy HQ preparatory to taking over work in tunnels	
	21		Work in tunnels carried on the usual until all work handed over to 103rd Field Coy RE, 24th Division. Coy marches back to BURGOMASTER'S FARM	OHR

A6945 Wt. W14422/M1160 350,000 12/16 D. D. & L. Forms/C./2118/14.

Army Form C. 2118.

WAR DIARY
or
INTELLIGENCE SUMMARY.
(Erase heading not required.)

76

102nd Field Coy RE

Instructions regarding War Diaries and Intelligence Summaries are contained in F. S. Regs., Part II. and the Staff Manual respectively. Title pages will be prepared in manuscript.

Place	Date	Hour	Summary of Events and Information	Remarks and references to Appendices
DICKEBUSCH	22	8 am	Coy. moved out & Transport lines at BURGOMASTER'S FARM & proceeded to rest billets in the BERTHEN Area.	DvR.
BERTHEN AREA	23		Camp routine, cleaning up etc. 2 Lieut C.D. SCAMMELL RE (T.C) joins Coy.	DvR.
	24		do.	
	25		Kit inspection. Heavy rain all day.	DvR.
ZUTOVE	26		Coy. moved out of billets from BERTHEN, ultaria at CAESTRE attain at ST OMER and moved to billets at ZUTOVE near BOISDINGHEM	DvR.
	27		TRANSPORT proceed by road to EBBLINGHEM for the night. 2 Lieut B.F. CLAYMER R.E. proceeds on leave to the U.K.	DvR.
	28		Camp fatigues. Transport moved from EBBLINGHEM to ZUTOVE.	DvR.
	29		Section Drill - Camp Fatigues	
LUMBRES	30		Coy. moved out of billets in ZUTOVE to billets at VAL DE LUMBRES. Coy H.Q. at LUMBRES	DvR.
	31		4 Sections at work on Rifle Range Construction at VAL DE LUMBRES for II Army.	DvR.

D.M. Rodd. Major R.E.
O.C. 102 F.U Coy RE

Army Form C. 2118.

WAR DIARY
or
INTELLIGENCE SUMMARY.
(Erase heading not required.)

(77) 102nd Field Coy. R.E. Vol 23

Place	Date	Hour	Summary of Events and Information	Remarks and references to Appendices
	1917 AUGUST			
LUMBRES	1–7		Coy at work on Rifle Range for 2nd Army at VAL DE LUMBRES	DwR
VLAMERTINGHE area	8		Coy (Divnl Postn) leave trestles at LUMBRES & proceed by Motor Busses to field near VLAMERTINGHE – YPRES road to work for XVIII corps on forward roads. MG portion of Coy proceed by road from LUMBRES to NORDPEENE. (Capt KIGELL R.E.) 2nd Lieut CAYMER returns from leave.	DwR
	9		C.E. XVIII corps comes round to look at roads to see Coy	DwR
	10		Coy (with C Coy 2 S Staffs) attack work on BUFFS ROAD. Working hours 8 – 12, 12.30 to 2.30 pm	DwR
			MG portion of Coy proceed by road from NORDPEENE to three miner.	
VLAMERTINGHE – POPERINGHE road	11		Work on Roads in Forward Area. Capt KIGELL R.E. sent to C.R.E's HQ as 2/Adjutant whilst Lieut SAUNDERS, Adjt R.E. is on leave. 2nd Lieut BAXTER T. James – Coy in Capt KIGELL'S place.	DwR
			No 47840 Lce Cpl KAIN A, No 51076 Spr LEES W, No 203718 Spr MOORE W, No 51061 Spr NEWBOLD C.A, Sp No 25172 Spr WILLIS W, wounded whilst were in trenches on forward roads.	

WAR DIARY or INTELLIGENCE SUMMARY

Army Form C. 2118.

(78)

102nd Field Coy RE 1917

Place	Date	Hour	Summary of Events and Information	Remarks and references to Appendices
	AUGUST			
VLAMERTINGHE	12		Work on BUFFS ROAD continued	
	13			AMR
	14		Work on BUFFS ROAD. Billets shelled at 4 p.m. & 7 p.m.	AMR
	15		No 59263 Spr Bennett R, No 25203 Spr Hayne S.W. wounded	AMR
	16		XVIII Corps allow Sect I (2 huts C.D. SCAMMELL R.E.) and 1 Proton S Staffs	AMR
			sent up to relieve BUFFS ROAD Work ADMIRALS ROAD & ST JULIEN ROAD	
			and keep it in a state of repair during the day. No. 53044 L/Cpl.	
			McDowell R., No 51640 Spr Princippo F.B. wounded.	
	17		Work on BUFFS ROAD (from ADMIRALS ROAD TO ST JULIEN ROAD)	AMR
	18		ditto	
	19			
	20			
	21		Work on BUFFS ROAD (as above) Interrupted by Shell Fire. 2 Lieut HENYE	AMR
			M.C. No 143923 Spr Galvin C.J., No 62578 Spr Luence F.W., No 51120 Spr.	
			Polkinghorne T wounded. No 93724 Spr. Hutchinson G wounded	

Army Form C. 2118.

WAR DIARY
or
INTELLIGENCE SUMMARY.
(Erase heading not required.)

102nd Field Coy. RE

1917

Instructions regarding War Diaries and Intelligence Summaries are contained in F. S. Regs., Part II. and the Staff Manual respectively. Title pages will be prepared in manuscript.

(7)

Place	Date AUGUST	Hour	Summary of Events and Information	Remarks and references to Appendices
VLAMERTINGHE Area	22		Work on Forward Roads (BUFFS ROAD & ADMIRALS ROAD) for	
	23		C.E. XVIII Corps	DYR
	24			
	25		Hand over work to 58th Division (505 Field Coy RE).	
DICKEBUSCH	26		March out of VLAMERTINCHE to huts near DICKEBUSCH,	DYR
			Take over work area from 85th Field Coy RE, 14th Division II Corps	
	27		Camp Fatigues etc	
	28		Work in Back Area including repairs to HUSSARS CAMP, construction of Baths	DYR
	29		Work on Corps & Div. R.E. Dumps, marking out P.g.W. Track from ZILLEBEKE	
			near to Camps DOA.	
	30		2nd Lieut J.A. LEECE. RE joins Coy. works in Back Area as above	DYR
	31		Works in Back Area.	

D.A. Robb. Major RE
O.C. 102nd Field Coy RE.

Army Form C. 2118.

WAR DIARY
or
INTELLIGENCE SUMMARY.
(Erase heading not required.)

102 Field Coy R.E.

1917

Place	Date SEPTEMBER.	Hour	Summary of Events and Information	Remarks and references to Appendices
DICKEBUSCH	1		Works in Bass Area (Construction of Dirt, Batts, roads at various Corps & Divl R.E. Dumps)	DYR.
	2		Camp bombed by aeroplane. Three horses wounded.	
	3		Reconnoitred forward Trench with C.R.E. 24th Divn. Major ROBB proceeded on leave to U.K.	
	4		Company came back by march route to X 9 δ 3.7 near METEREN.	
			Vicinity of this Camp bombed by aeroplane. No casualties	
	5–9		In rest. One horse doll dead.	
	10		Company moved up entrained in field at H 34 c 3.6 (Sheet 28)	
	11 12 13 14		took preparing Divl H.Q. at BURGOMASTER'S FARM DICKEBUSCH. 25 NISSEN huts put up with some help from 103 Field Co. N5. G.O.C. 23rd Div Theurched the Company for work done.	
	15		Major ROBB returned from leave. No 3 Section bathing on Div A.Q. Remainder of Co. bathing in Camp. Capt KIGGELL went to Epis to Barathon office.	
	16–23		Carried works at Div HQ, road huts, etc. Drainage St Div Baths on Brigade HQ at Bedford House etc	DYR.

DICKEBUSCH Mator Barry

WAR DIARY
INTELLIGENCE SUMMARY

Army Form C. 2118.

(81)

102nd Field Coy. R.E.

1917

Place	Date	Hour	Summary of Events and Information	Remarks and references to Appendices
DICKEBUSCH	SEPT 24		Left camp at DICKEBUSCH & march via B field here LA CLYTTE. CAPT RIDSDILL rejoins Coy from R.E. H.Q.	DWR
LA CLYTTE	25		Making camp &c. Work on horse standings under CRE II Corps	DWR
"	26		Troops Work on horse standings &c	DWR
	27		do. CAPT J RIDSDILL goes on leave to U.K.	
	28		do. 2 Lieut LONG-ANDERSON goes on leave to S.France	DWR
	29		Work on forward road (PLUMER DRIVE South to CLAPHAM JUNCTION) under CRE 23 Div.	DWR
	30		do.	

D.J. Roth, Major R.E.
O.C. 102 Fld Coy R.E.

Army Form C. 2118.

WAR DIARY
or
INTELLIGENCE SUMMARY.

(Erase heading not required.)

102nd Field Coy. R.E.

WM 2425

Place	Date	Hour	Summary of Events and Information	Remarks and references to Appendices
	OCTOBER			
LA CLYTTE	1		Work on northern road from PLUMER DRIVE through SANCTUARY WOOD	SWR
	2 & 3		To CLAPHAM JUNCTION	SWR
	4		do	SWR
	5		Under orders CRE X Corps Troops	
	6		Work on BEATTY & JELLICOE Comm Dumps (near CAFE BELGE) & Tilleloy	SWR
	7		in SCOTTISH & RIDGE woods, now Troops at IRON BRIDGE, 2	SWR
EIZENWALLE	8		do Capt. J. RIDDELL returns from leave	
	9		do 2 Lieut W.C.HAND-ANDERSON returns from leave	SWR
	10		do 2 Lieut E.F. BAXTER proceeds on escort to U.K.	
	11		Moved out of Camp at LA CLYTTE to huts in RIDGE WOOD. Take over work	
RIDGE WOOD	12		in T.K. line (CHENCORSE WOOD to REUTEL Water) from 97th Field Coy RE	SWR
	13		Commence work on tracks from CHENCORSE WOOD to POLYGONEWOOD to REUTEL. Work on tram as above. Nos 48964 L.Cpl LUCAS W. (Mine owner), 552802 Spr.	SWR
			SMITH J., 145335 HOWELL F.P., 51011 BIGNELL A. wounded & all others	SWR
	14		Work on Tracks & Wedge (post) POLYGONEWEEN. 2 Lieut I.A. LEECE RE evacuated over	SWR

A6945 Wt. W14422/M1160 350000 12/16 D. D. & L. Forms/C./2118/14.

Army Form C. 2118.

WAR DIARY
or
INTELLIGENCE SUMMARY.

(Erase heading not required.)

102nd Field Coy R.E. (83)

1917

Instructions regarding War Diaries and Intelligence Summaries are contained in F. S. Regs., Part II. and the Staff Manual respectively. Title pages will be prepared in manuscript.

Place	Date	Hour	Summary of Events and Information	Remarks and references to Appendices
	OCTOBER			
RIDGE WOOD	15		Work on Tracks.	O.u.R.
	16		do. 30356 A/L Stephens W. 92055 S/L Townshend E. wounded	
	17		do.	O.u.R.
	18		Work on Tracks. 2 Lieut R.F.T. Blewitt R.E. joins W Coy	
	19		do. 2 Lieut R.F.T. Blewitt R.E. Transferred to 101 Fld Coy R.E.	
	20		Work on Tracks	
	21		Work on Tracks. Hand over work on Tracks to 126th Fld Coy R.E. Capt. T. Kiggell R.E. leaves Coy on appointment to command 400th Field Coy R.E. Lieut T. Huckstep R.E. appointed 2nd in Command 102 Coy + joins Coy for duty	O.u.R.
BOESHEPE area	22		Coy marches on to Arretto in RIDGE WOOD + inings in X Corps School BOESHEPE area. 2 Lieut E.E. Baxter returns from leave.	O.u.R.
	23		Coy work on X Corps Schools under C.R.E. X Corps Troops	
	24		do	

A6945 Wt. W11422/M160 350,000 12/16 D. D. & L. Forms/C/2118/14.

WAR DIARY
or
INTELLIGENCE SUMMARY.
(Erase heading not required.)

Army Form C. 2118.

(84)

102 Field Coy RE

1917

Place	Date	Hour	Summary of Events and Information	Remarks and references to Appendices
	OCTOBER.			
BOESHEPE	25		Work on X Corps Schools	SMR
	26		do	
	27		do	SMR
	28		Reserve notice to stand by for entraining	
	29		Work on X Corps Schools	SMR
	30		Checking equipment etc	SMR
	31		Coy Training	

D.T. Ross Major RE
O.C. 102 Field Coy RE.

www.ingramcontent.com/pod-product-compliance
Lightning Source LLC
Chambersburg PA
CBHW081551160426
43191CB00011B/1902